This is th
while I

THE
BROKEN
TRUTH

I said I would put his face on the front cover.
He said "No Karl" in a strong voice!
Put my cross and break it, dark clouds and just three
ray's coming down on the cross from the sun.
These are the Trinity, God, the Son Jesus Christ
and the Holy Spirit, Amen: (Powerful)

ISBN 978-1-64079-781-9 (paperback)
ISBN 978-1-64079-782-6 (digital)

Christian Faith Publishing, Inc.
832 Park Avenue
Meadville, PA 16335
www.christianfaithpublishing.com

Printed in the United States of America

The Broken Truth

KARL OLSON

INTRODUCTION

This is a book about my life. It's a story the Lord wants out there. It's about my struggles and how I overcame them through adversity with all the challenges I have. It's about my four miracles the Lord did for me. It's a story about how God can work in your life if you let him. This happened so many years ago, but I have never forgotten it. Every day, the Lord has inspired me to write this book for the last year and a half. So here it is. I hope this story helps whoever is reading it and I believe it will if you pray and ask the Lord to help you. The story will show how good the Lord can be. We only need to ask.

In the beginning of our life, no one knows what kind of life we are going to live. We're born in an unexpected world. We can't pick and choose the life we want. We are destined how we are when we're born with the type of family we live with and everything around us. As we grow up, it's up to us as to what we are going to be. This whole life is a test to see if we're going to follow the Lord or not. It's up to you if you want to be good or bad. You decide your own outcome. Jesus gave us that right for deep down in our hearts we know right from wrong. God's laws are written within us. Our own conscience accuses us. (Rom. 2:13)

Jesus died on the cross over 2,000 years ago. Yes, he did, and he is alive today. I believe in his Word because there are so many lessons we can learn from the Bible. It is real. Pick it up and read it. Don't let that Bible sit anymore in dust at your home. Pick it up, and have an open heart when you do. You could just say a simple prayer to yourself before you open the Bible. Say teach me, Lord, your word. Have a sincere attitude and an open mind. The Bible is meant for everyone in this whole world.

CHAPTER 1

The Challenges of Having a Stern Father

I was born the youngest of four kids, and I had no idea all the challenges I would face when I grew up. I was born with weak eye muscles in both eyes and one of my eyes kept wandering. My mom said eventually I needed eye surgery but they had to wait until I became three because my eyes needed to be more mature before they could do surgery. I remember seeing double vision on the TV set, and my mom said when I was little, I would hold my head and say my tummy hurt.

I went to the hospital at age three and was scared to death because I had to spend the night there. I saw my parents leaving the hospital in the elevator. I ran out of my room into the hallway. I hit the elevator with my hands and some lady come out and put me back into bed. I kept saying I want my mommy and I cried myself to sleep. I guess parents couldn't stay in those days plus my dad had to go back to work, but I didn't understand that. When I came home from the hospital, I had to do eye exercises with a patch on my eye and then switch the patch from left to right. One exercise was to hold a stick far away from my face while I moved it slowly toward my nose and I had to keep my eyes focused on it. I also had to wear glasses with red and blue lenses. Then I could do eye drawings on paper.

I also needed regular eye glasses. Now at the young age of three, I had to learn to be responsible … glasses are important. I had to watch and be very careful with them, not to sit or step on them. My dad was very particular about that.

When my dad walked into a room, you guarded your behavior. If you were doing wrong, he knew. Our dad was a very orderly and organized man. He knew if something was out of place, and we all learned facial expressions at an early age. He didn't have to say much and we knew he meant business. He was also a very serious man. He was never a silly or goofy man. Our dad was from the Old School—he was very strict. He was not your buddy. When I was real little, I remember the word NO and the snap of his finger … and he never wavered on discipline. He believed in consistency. Once he said something, he stayed with it. He never changed his mind, he believed consistency is the best policy. He believed in tough love. He was not an emotional man—we never saw him cry ever in front of us. He put that away years ago because his dad died when he was fourteen years old. His older sister and two older brothers were gone so he had to be a man and grow up fast which required him to get a job to help support his mom and younger sister. We were never allowed to walk into our parent's bedroom. We had to knock first. We never slept with our parents even when we were scared during thunderstorms. Our dad would say, "Go back upstairs. You'll be all right."

Karl's family: Front row-Dad (Gerald) & Mom (Maxine)
Back row L to R-Paul, Jeff, Jenny & Karl

I remember my dad coming home from a hard day's work and being very tired. You know how kids can be ... how we test our parents. Well, it didn't matter how tired he was laying on the couch with his eyes closed. When we looked out the window with our finger touching the window or watching TV too closely or touching our white walls in our house, he would still snap his finger and say NO.

We were raised at Bayview Wesleyan Church and were taught that church was a must. I believe it's very important for parents to teach and make their children go to church. For it says in the Bible, *"Train up a child in the way he should go and when he is old he will not depart from it."* (Prov. 22:6)

We can remember this song in church: "Jesus loves me this I know for the Bible tells me so! Little ones to him belong.

"They are weak but he is strong. Yes, Jesus loves me, yes, Jesus loves me, and yes, Jesus loves me for the Bible tells me so." Jesus loves EVERYONE! I believe the Bible is very important if we would just pick it up! We would find many clues in it. For instance: Read Luke 16:19-31.

There was a certain rich man, Jesus said, "who was splendidly clothed and lived each day in mirth and luxury. One day, Lazarus, a diseased beggar, was laid at his door. As he lay there longing for scraps from the rich man's table, the dogs would come and lick his open sores. Finally, the beggar died and was carried by the angels to be with Abraham in the place of the righteous dead. The rich man also died and was buried, and his soul went into hell. There in torment, he saw Lazarus in the far distance with Abraham. 'Father Abraham,' he shouted, 'have some pity! Send Lazarus over here if only to dip the tip of his finger in water and cool my tongue, for I am in anguish in these flames.' But Abraham said to him, 'Son, remember that during your lifetime you had everything you wanted, and Lazarus had nothing. So now he is here being comforted and you are in anguish. And besides, there is a great chasm separating us, and anyone wanting to come to you from here is stopped at its edge; and no one over there can cross to us.' Then the rich man said, 'O, Father Abraham, then please send him to my father's home for I have five brothers to warn them about this place of torment lest they come here when they die.' But Abraham said, 'The scriptures have warned them again and again. Your brothers can read them any time they want to.' The rich man replied, 'No, Father Abraham, they won't bother to read them. But if someone is sent to them from the dead, then they will turn from their sins.' But Abraham said, 'O,' they won't listen to Moses and the prophets, they won't listen even though someone rises from the dead."

Notice the rich man said, *"If only to dip the tip of his finger in water and cool my tongue."* Do we need to experience this anguish in hell forever before it's too late with how we live down here? This is why we need to pick up the Bible and read it … let's notice this about others that need our help and are struggling in life. Our parents also believe (just like you) Fear God as you should fear your parents. They also said you should have a well-balanced life … even food all things in moderation. You have church in your life as well as public school; too … You need to be part of the world but not of the world. You need to experience the challenges. How other people are, exposed to others but not act like them, let the Lord be your guide.

When I was five, I was learning to ride my tricycle. I would ride down the block from my house. I had a speech problem and needed speech therapy for several years after this. Anyway, there were three teenagers across the other side of the intersection sitting on their front porch and they were yelling at me, "What's your name?" and I couldn't pronounce my name right! So two of them ran across the road and asked again. They just came up to me and flipped my tricycle out from under me. I skinned my elbow and my knee on the sidewalk. As I was bleeding, I thought, "What did I do to you?" So I ran home crying and told my mom what happened. My oldest brother, Paul, was the only one home with my mom. She sent him out to help me get my tricycle back. He's eight years older than me. So he went with me to retrieve the tricycle. He also took care of the two teenagers. The other one stayed on the porch.

I watched him and was so amazed. I'm thinking, "WOW! My big brother, Paul, helped me."

I remember getting a shot at the doctor's office when I was little. I didn't want one! Every time the doctor would try, I would twist my body and say no! Next thing I know, my dad opened the door of the office. He didn't say a word but just stared at me. I froze. He had this serious look on his face! I'm thinking, "Oh, no." Then the doctor gave me a shot in the arm. Later, I nervously asked my dad why he had to come in there. My dad looked at me sternly and said, "Because the doctor doesn't get paid to deal with your tantrum! He's got a job to do and you're supposed to let him do his job!" I never forgot that—he's right! Even at the dentist's office, just open your mouth and don't squirm. Do what you're told! Sit there and let them do their job! Our parents will get the word about how we just sat there and was orderly … or not.

It was 1968, and we went on a family trip out west for a four-week vacation. We had a four-door car pulling a pop-up Apache camper that slept six of us. We followed behind our cousins in their big trailer. There were six of them too. We drove down through Michigan to Chicago, Illinois, up to Wisconsin to Minnesota. We went to South Dakota and saw Mount Rushmore and Crazy Horse Statue and drove around up in the Black Hills where they blasted holes in the cliffs so you could drive your car right through them. We traveled through the badlands and went to Wall Drugs. Then we finely got to Wyoming where we saw Devil's Tower National Monument. We also went to Yellowstone National Park. While there, we saw bears on the main road. People were throwing their bread bags out for the bears to eat. Dad had some, too. We watched the bears rip open the sacks and devour the bread.

We then spent time camping and decided to go down to Jackson Hole, Wyoming where Dad got us cowboy hats. On the way back, we stopped to look at the Grand Teton Mountain. While I looked at the mountain, I was thinking how majestic the Lord is and powerful too! WOW! While we were there, we saw prairie dogs all over the place. There were hundreds of them at Cunningham Cabins. We had never seen them before!

Returning to our campsite in Yellowstone Park, we saw the geysers the next morning. There were certain areas where you could walk. My brother, Jeff, who's four years older than me, had his hat blow off his head. He ran off the trail to catch his hat. Our dad yelled at him, "Jeff! Stop Right There!" He froze in place. I was six at the time but never forgot that incident. That's how much authority our dad had over us. When he said something, we listened RIGHT NOW! Our dad carried himself in a serious manner—even on vacation. If Jeff had stepped one or two steps more, we would have lost him. He would have fallen in the boiling water.

We stayed at camp a few days more so we could see other things. I remember one day, I heard a scream for help. My dad went running up to the laundry but told me to stay right there in the camp. It was my brother, Jeff, who got his hand caught in one of those old wringers. He was okay and just had a little mark on his arm.

From there, we left for Montana to Glacier National Park, up on Logan's Pass. We saw lots of animals up there. From there, we went up to Canada, through British

Columbia and up to the Glacier Mountains. There were lots of mountain goats on the side of the mountain. We took lots of pictures on our video camera. We were going to go to Jasper to ride the tram, but it was too foggy. So we decided to head for home. We traveled on the Canadian roads and back in 1968, they weren't that good. We finally got to Sault Ste. Marie, crossed the bridge into Michigan, and went on down to the Mackinac Bridge and then home to Traverse City.

CHAPTER 2

Enduring the Emotional
Rollercoaster of Being Different

We were home within a month before I had to get ready for school to begin. I was going into kindergarten. My mom had a tradition of buying a sleeping mat for us and having us stand on the front porch for a picture before we left for school. Our names were written on the back of the mats in black magic marker along with our address. I also remember my sister, Jenny, getting her mat. Our parents started us in school when we were six. I guess we would be a little older. Anyway, I couldn't handle kindergarten because I couldn't stay focused. When the teacher left the room, some of the kids would get up off their mats and run around. I would be the farthest away from my sleeping mat when the teacher would walk into the room and I got caught off my mat. And when she would be telling the class a story, I would speak out of turn which got me sent to the principal's office so many times that I got kicked out of kindergarten and sent to a Child Guidance Clinic Center where they diagnosed me with ADD or Attention Deficit Disorder. I couldn't concentrate; my attention span was off from the regular kids. I didn't understand this at all. So this new teacher had me do a lot of puzzles like blocks I had to put together. One puzzle I had to put the circle in the circle hole, the square in the square hole and so on. I was timed and they had a one-way mirror that your parent could watch you, but you didn't see them.

So the counselor told my parents that I had a low-IQ but when they timed me, they said I can grow it because I was improving more. He also noticed that my parents (Dad) balanced each other out when it came to me for there strictness and love. I also had to take medicine (Ritalin) and had to go to a special school for special kids that had problems like this. I felt a little unfamiliar with this and uncomfortable. "Why am I in here with them?" But I also knew I could keep up with everyone. I stayed on top of this class so I felt pretty good about that. But I had a hard time with the regular kids getting on the bus for school. Kids were mean. I got called four eyes, and I saw kids picking on other kids also like putting their heads in the snow bank. When I got on the bus, kids would snap their finger on the back of my ears. So through the years in grade school, I dealt with regular kids that didn't understand me because I was different. I was quiet and reserved. So just because I was slow, they would pick on me. I remember talking about this to my dad and he always told me the principle to every action there is a reaction. He would say, "Just don't respond and it will go away." Well, it never seemed to. It went on for months. I told dad that I'm going to hit back! My dad would say, "Nope. Two wrongs don't make a right!" I heard this lot … turn the other cheek (Matt. 5:39); remember in the Bible.

When our dad got home in the evening from work, we always got together as a family in our dining room to eat dinner at 6:00 p.m. Our dad would tell our mom or us kids to say grace before we ate and we always ate what was on the table. Our dad didn't go for being goofy at the table, and he didn't believe in waste. If you didn't like your food, you couldn't get a bowl of cereal. You HAD TO EAT what was on your plate! Sunday was family day—we all stayed home.

Our family never lived on any kind of assistance. Dad was a very proud worker—a hard worker—who worked at the post office. He worked long hours and wasn't home much. He worked five to six days per week. Christmas was the worst time of year for him. He didn't get home until late evening from work and he worked twelve to fourteen hours per day. He was very stressed and tired. We got snow in October, and it stayed all winter which didn't help because he was a rural mail carrier. He had to peddle mail in lots of snow with his GMC truck. Then later on, he worked in the office as a General Foreman. So he was gone a lot but he was almost always home for discipline—if we needed it! In Proverbs 19:18, it says, *"Discipline your son in his early years while there is hope. If you don't, you will ruin his life."* Yes kids were not just kids (we were a well reserved family). You didn't have the run of the house. We had new furniture and was taught respect for it. You couldn't just plop on the couch. And our dad didn't believe in child proofing the house. You had to learn not to touch certain stuff. We all lived on his one paycheck from work. His first financial obligation was his tithes for the Lord … 10%. He had twenty-six years perfect attendance and served thirty-four years with the post office. He was never late and didn't believe in being sick. Being late was like a sin and our dad taught us that.

Now, our mom is a great mother. She is the home-maker in our family. She did all the cooking, cleaning, and dusting all around the house. Each morning, she would call each of us by name to get up and ready for school. She had our breakfast hot and ready every morning. She made pancakes and eggs, hot oatmeal, or Malt-O-Meal. She packed our lunches for school too! Mom was able to do this because our dad worked. At night, us kids all had certain times to go to bed depending on our age. Being the youngest, I had to go to bed before all of the rest. So Mom would read a story book to us before she tucked each one of us to bed and taught us our prayers every night. She is so loving and caring; we appreciate her very much. When I was little I remember praying by myself upstairs on my knees in my bedroom and I felt the presences of the Lord. Like he was right there leaning over my bed and I said to Him "I surrender all to you Jesus" and I asked Him if he could use me for his purpose...

At Christmas time, we had a couple catalogs to look at to find what we were wanting. One was a Sear's Wish Book, and we could only pick one gift for Christmas. Our stockings were full hanging on the fireplace. But before we could see our gifts, we always had Pop Tarts and hot cocoa for Christmas breakfast and a five-course dinner later that evening. So our Christmas was wonderful as well as Easter and on our birthday.

We celebrated Easter and on our birthday, our mom would ask us what we would like for dinner and what kind of cake we wanted. We all had nice presents for our birthday. Rarely did we go out to eat but when we did, you'd see people come up to the table and say "O sir, Mr., I want to say how nice it is to see your kids like little quiet soldiers at attention. They sit right there nice and quiet, all four kids. They don't run around and get in your way so I want to compliment you." I'm thinking I know why!

Our second road trip was in 1970. We went on vacation with just the six of us for a month to the lower southwest states with our Apache camper. We went through Indiana, Illinois, Missouri, Oklahoma, and Texas. In Texas, I remember Jenny and I were at some playground where we stopped. We were swinging on a swing set that had red fire ants everywhere. Of course they had to sting us. Then we went through New Mexico into Arizona to see the Petrified Forest, Painted Desert, and Meteor Crater. From there, we went back down to White Sands in Alamogordo, New Mexico, and Carl Bad Caverns.

We went back through Arizona to see the Grand Canyon and Hoover Dam where we stayed at Lake Mead, and I remember diving over and over which is what I did at a local pool in Traverse City. I kept diving and didn't realize I had gone past the buoy. I wasn't a good swimmer and I was in over my head. I thought, "Oh no, I was scared." I kept jumping up and grabbing the buoy but I couldn't hang on and kept going down to the bottom of the lake. I would push myself up with my feet. I did this three times and every time I did, I kept yelling for help! No one seemed to be around! I said to myself, this is it! After the third time, I yelled for help, some guy came and grabbed me. I really came close to drowning that day. Through the years,

I thought there must be a reason I'm still here. The Lord must want me here for a reason.

After that, we decided to go through Nevada to California but it was too hot. It was 120 degrees in the shade and we didn't have air conditioning in our car. We had another sixty miles to get to the California border. It was just too hot! There were miles and miles of hot, hot, hot desert! So we decided to go to the upper states instead. Up in the cooler state of Idaho and on the way home, we went through Wyoming, Nebraska, Iowa, Illinois, Indiana, and Michigan to home. I never forgot that. WOW!

When we got home, we had some new neighbors that had moved in. My new friend, Mark, had trains and racing cars in his basement and we had a lot of fun hanging out!

In 1972, our family helped our grandma Ila Olson move up here from Cleveland, Ohio, to Traverse City, because her brother Paul had died. We had the funeral up here because they we're from here. That same year my brother, Paul, graduated from high school.

Karl at 10

My dad's brother, Ray, is a carpenter and he helped my dad remodel the garage into a little house behind our house. We lived at 201 N. Madison and we called our grandma's house 201 1/2 N. Madison in 1972.

Our dad is a very smart man. He knows all about wire codes for the electric in her little home. He knows plumbing, how to fix a car. He wasn't a mechanic but he was mechanically inclined. That is rare ... not a lot of mechanics have this ability. He also knows a lot about medicine since he worked at a pharmacy before going to work at the post office. So he knew about pharmacology. Our dad was like a sponge. He would learn how to do things just by reading in a book. I remember him fixing the old TV tubes on the back of the TV set.

When my grandma moved here, she didn't have a very good retirement check. So my dad helped out with his own money to pay expenses so she could live a better life.

CHAPTER 3

Suffering the Pain of Being Bullied

Going back to school and dealing with those regular kids was hard to do. It always seemed like I was born with a target on my back. I was the one to be picked on and wasn't respected. Most of the time kids on the bus would say, "Don't sit here!" And one kid said the reason I pick on you is because you look like you deserve it. That's why I do it. It seemed the nicer I was with kids, the meaner they got. My self-esteem seemed really low, and I didn't understand this at all. This was really traumatic, being called four eyes. I was really bothered by this. After months of being picked on, I finally turned around and asked that kid if he could please stop picking on me. He punched me in the mouth and gave me a bloody lip. I walked off the school bus and felt really bad. Later, I cried on my way home.

When I had problems, my mom told me to wait an hour after your father comes home so he can rest awhile and read his newspaper. Then you can tell him. I waited for an hour then I told him. My dad said, "You were wrong. I told you don't react! Don't respond! Ignore him. Keep your mouth closed! It will go away!" I said to myself, "Lord, there must be a reason for this." Here are some helpful words from the Bible that we need to listen to.

John 16:3: *"I have told you all this so that you will have peace of heart and mind. Here on earth you will have many trials and sorrows; but cheer up for I have overcome the world."* I live by that verse. Thank you, Lord!

Romans 8:28: *"And we know that all that happens to us is working for our good if we love God and are fitting into his plans."*

You see, it says all that happens to us. It doesn't necessarily say good. It can be bad but it's working for our good if we love God and are fitting into his plans. Through my grade school years when we got out of school, our mom sent us to summer Vacation Bible School at our church. I loved going there because we made crafts and did all kinds of things. Then when we were a few years older, we went to CYC at church. I even had two or three buttons on my sash for learning Bible verses. I remember my brother, Jeff, had thirty-five to fifty on his. I thought that was great!

Sixth grade was tough. I'm not sure what happened but some teacher said I wasn't ready to move up to seventh grade. So they held me back in sixth grade for another year. Apparently, I had difficulty controlling my emotions, and I couldn't stay focused. I would talk out of turn. I needed to be put back on medication (Ritalin).

My dad told me that when I turned twelve it would be the last year to go trick or treating. And when he said something, he stayed with it. So when I was thirteen years old, I had to pass out candy at my parent's home. I really wanted to go out because I heard other kids in school saying they were going out. I didn't dare argue. Well, I was passing out candy to some of these kids that were bigger than me. They must have been sixteen years old. I told my dad, "Did you see that? These kids are bigger than me." He said, "Never mind about them. I'm telling you. You are not responsible for them. You are only responsible for yourself." Oh boy, how many times did I hear this!

O, dear Lord, my self-esteem is really low. I've always felt really bad because I had to take sixth grade over again. I didn't know what I'm good at. There must be something that I'm good at. What is it, Lord? Our family liked to have all of us kids to have musical talents and I just don't understand how to follow notes. My parents never pushed me to learn music because they knew how I was. But I felt bad because I couldn't. My brother, Paul, played guitar. My brother, Jeff, played violin and my sister, Jenny, played piano. And they were all really good at it!

Since I was staying another year in sixth grade, I remember watching my dad play chess with my older brothers. So through my childhood years, I asked my dad if he would teach me how to play chess. I thought that was neat because I got to spend quality time with my dad and he beat me quite a lot in chess, but I was getting better at it. I was starting to beat him now and then and he told me that he was really trying to beat me.

When we had recess time in school, there was a chess set sitting on a table in the library. So I sat there and kids wanted to play chess with me. I played quite a lot of kids. I surprised some of them. I would checkmate them in four moves. Some of the kids couldn't believe it! I was feeling pretty good about myself but I was never conceited. I was always nice to others. I was declared chess champion in sixth grade. Thank you, Dad and Mom.

In sixth grade, we had a class about drugs and they showed a film strip on how it affects our body and our mind. They had a slogan—"Say NO to Drugs!" Well, I already made up my mind on this because drugs kill brain cells and *I need all I have*! I already feel like I'm behind everyone else so I say no to drugs and also drinking alcohol too! Also in sixth grade, I did safety patrol and wore a white safety belt for training. There was one guy who wore a yellow belt with a lieutenant badge on. He came out and was walking off the white line in the road acting like he was drunk. I would yell at him and tell him to not to walk off the white line. Of course I couldn't talk right and said Lion instead of line. Well, he kept bothering me and yelling at me, "Lion, lion, What is lion?" There were some other kids that wanted to give me drugs. I said with a sharp and quick voice, "I say no to drugs." Later, I received my yellow belt.

One day, I was home with my parents in the living room. My dad said to me, "What do you say when someone approaches you about drug?" I looked at him and said with a quick stern voice, "I Say NO to Drugs!" My dad and mom were impressed, and you could see it on their faces. Well, I simply said, "I don't want drugs in my life because it kills brain cells and I need all that I have."

Through my childhood years and on, I loved going over to my grandma's house. She always seemed to be in good spirits and I had a lot of fun talking to her. She always had little knickknack candy around and she loved to collect owl figurines. I loved to run over there to give her hugs. We all loved going to her little house and playing games.

We played Triominos, Sorry, Yahtzee, Triple Yahtzee, and other card games. She was so good at beating us too … She also loved the Lord in her life … I remember on the weekends she would have all these older ladies come over to her house. She would have big Bunko parties and had prizes to win. She also had Tupperware parties. Sometimes, one of the ladies would be sick and my sister, Jenny, would get to go over there and play as a substitute. She usually came home winning prizes too. She had so much fun and I was so happy and so proud of her. My grandma never swore. If she got mad, she would only say two words: "Oh Fudge or oh fiddlesticks!" Cute!

That spring, during my seventh grade year at home, I decided to train a wild squirrel in my backyard! I named him Peanuts. I would throw shelled peanuts at him far away and each day just a little closer until he would trust me. Eventually, he would feed right out of my hand. I thought this was one of God's wonderful little creatures! Eventually, I got him to climb up my leg running all around me like a tree and up to my shoulder to the top of my head. And he'd call all his friends, too! So I fed them also—for two years … then after that, somebody ran him over in a car down the road. I lost my interest after that. Thank you, Lord, for this moment of joy! I love Peanuts!

In the fall before school, started I got braces when I was thirteen because my teeth were crooked and I had to wear a retainer at night to help line up my jaw. I remember that summer just before my brother, Jeff, entered seventh grade when I was eight. We walked eight miles round trip just to go see the new school. They had just built the new building for seventh, eighth, and ninth grade junior high school. He was excited to show me around before he started that year. I was excited about entering seventh grade four years after him but at the same time nervous because all the classes looked tough. So I needed special classes because I couldn't keep up with the regular kids. For some reason, I was comfortable in Mrs. Woods class, (Room 224) and some other special classes like Shroeger's room because before that there was one regular class I had in sixth grade

Feeding Peanuts with friends
Eric & Phillip

I really struggled with. I remember taking an exam or test and out of thirty kids I was the last one done! Talk about peer pressure! But going in the seventh grade was a lot better on the school buses. They had new routes to get to school and the kids were a lot better than grade school kids. They left you alone! My whole seventh grade year, I never needed my medication again (I grew out of it).

My Special Ed teacher, Mrs. Woods, had that same look on her face like my father. You didn't push any farther or you would be in trouble. I also have a lot of respect for her. Sometimes, they would have a parent meeting conference about us kids and she would rave to me about my parents because she would tell them about my attitude and my parents (Dad) would say they would take care of it. A lot of other parents would say "not my kid." So when Dad said he would take care of it, there would be consequences for your actions! One morning, I went out to the kitchen to pour a cup of coffee for my dad and brought it for him sitting in the living room and my dad said in a sternly manner, that was very thoughtful, taking a sip of coffee "but very early" but you are still grounded! Oh my, I'm thinking to myself …

That spring we had the Special Olympics and I was pretty good at running. I won a lot of first place blue ribbons. So I felt pretty good about myself. When I got out of school from the seventh grade that following summer, I asked my dad for a raise in my allowance. My dad looked at me sternly for about five seconds, didn't say anything, then said, "You know what you need to do!" in a stern way. So in 1976 when I was fourteen years old, I went down to the Social Security office and got my work card. I worked inside the newspaper plant on the main floor stuffing ads and sections together that summer.

Meanwhile, I was learning to set my new alarm clock radio that my parents gave me for my birthday. My dad told me in a stern manner to make sure when that alarm goes off to get right up right away. He'd say, "Do not lie back down and push that snooze button." No matter how you feel! Get your butt up, get in there, and do not be late! Allow yourself plenty of time and make sure you get a little breakfast before starting your day!"

Back to school in the eighth grade our Special Ed. Teacher, Mrs. Woods, took all of us kids on a field trip to a skating rink. I had my ice skates on, walking in a slow-motion pace because I had weak ankles. I fell in an awkward way. My body was twisted and I broke my leg. Mrs. Woods thought I was faking it. So I went to get back up and fell again.

Then she realized I did have a problem. So during that year, I got a full leg cast almost all the way up to my groin. The teachers and classmates signed my cast. Mrs. Woods was so nice, she would pick me up for school every morning until I got my cast removed, and then I could ride the bus again. She would drive up to the front of our house and my mom made sure Mrs. Woods wasn't waiting on me. So I walked out there with my crutches.

Mrs. Woods had her dad who was a physical therapist, come into the classroom to teach me how to walk up and down stairs with my crutches. He brought a three step stool that I could train on. I was so thankful to him ... and Mrs. Woods was so wonderful.

Since I was on crutches for a while, I gained some weight in eighth grade. I was 5'7" and weighed 165 pounds. Well, one day one of my teachers said, "When you grow up, I can see you being a fat man." Well, that really bothered me. So that whole summer, I ran every day. I said to myself, "I'm going to show her." So I ran to be healthy and I also worked again at the newspaper business for the summer after school was out in 1977.

That fall, I started my ninth grade year in school and the teacher noticed I had lost weight. I lost twenty-five pounds and grew two inches taller that summer. She was shocked! So after my ninth grade was over, I worked at a restaurant doing dishes and rode my bike fourteen miles round trip all summer long. The restaurant was the one where my neighbor friend, Mark, worked. So he helped me get work there.

I was going into the tenth grade that fall. We had new buses and different routes. A whole new school again, I had three Special Ed classes and three regular classes; one was gym class. Now I struggled to get out of Special Ed. I said "there must be something I can do ..." in school, I was behind all the others. I couldn't keep up with the regular kids. I really felt cheated when it came to brains. I had many headaches when I studied all night at home for exams and some people are just born smart. So unfair ... I really wanted to be smarter and I asked myself many times, "Why Lord?" Kids would be so awful to me going in the Special Ed classes. When we had exams in regular classes, I would be the last one leaving. It felt like I was stuck between two worlds. When I was in Special Ed, I was the smartest one in there and when I was in regular classes, I was right at the bottom. I said to myself a lot of times, "Lord, why do I feel stuck in the middle?" My two older brothers and my older sister were all in regular classes in school. They were very smart in their classes. There was an SAT course for all kids when they got into tenth grade. My brothers and sister all scored 14th grade level and when I went into tenth grade, I scored seventh grade level! My IQ was 106.

In 1978, toward winter, we had our house fire. About 1:30 a.m., it started in the basement and the fire stayed down there because the firemen were called quickly. The fire chief was really pleased with my dad because he snow blowed with the snow blower all around the whole house like he did all winter long. So the firemen didn't have to walk in heavy snow and it was easy for them to lie down, break the window in the basement to put it out. However, there was about eighty thousand dollars in damages. The fire didn't get any farther than the basement but it almost broke through the first floor in the living room. But the firemen got it out in time although the kitchen was about to ignite! It was about 350 degrees in there, so it almost ignited but they saved it! But all the heavy black smoke ruined the whole house; it tarnished all the walls and everything else. The white walls became a creamy skin color. It was so hot in the kitchen, the microwave melted. Our dad had house insurance, so we were covered. I remember the next couple days going down in the basement. I looked up at the wood and it was all charcoal! I never forgot that smell of burnt wood in the house and the sulfur smell of smoke all through the house.

Anyway, when the fire happened, we all ran outside, and I forgot to get my hamsters. So I told my sister, Jenny, I was going to go back in. Next thing I know, my dad was yelling at me from the bottom of the stairs. As I was coming down from the second floor, he grabbed me and pulled me. I lost my balance and fell on top of him cracking two of his ribs but he was all right. However, I lost my hamsters.

Following the fire, we all stayed in the little house because my grandma was away in Florida. Now the contractor that worked for our insurance had to repaint the whole house, fix, and repair the new ceiling boards of the basement. Then they spayed that silver paint on the boards. Now my dad had to get really tough on them. He made some of them redo it over when they were hurrying to go to another job that was a commercial building with fire damage. So they left and my dad made them come back to finish the job correctly. Some of the doors weren't shutting because they had painted the doors without sanding them first.

CHAPTER 4

Finding My Purpose

During my tenth grade year, my gym teacher gave me an *A* for running in his gym class outside. I beat the whole class; I ran a 6:45 mile in under seven minutes. So he asked me if I wanted to join his track team after school for the Traverse City Trojans. I was flattered and said yes! I'm really thinking, "That's it, Lord. That's what I want to do! That's what I'm good at!" Now when I joined the junior varsity team, I was the worst runner on the team. And I'm thinking this is harder, this isn't Special Olympics either. This is regular track. They would have two captains who picked their teams. I would be the last one picked from the bench. I hated that and I'd say to myself, "Here we go again! I'm going to prove myself to them!" I also said, "God, I don't have the mental capacity but you gave me physical ability. But I have to train real hard just like everyone else because these regular kids aren't the same as special kids." I asked my dad if he could pick me up after track practice. He said "No" you are a young man with young leg's you can walk home. I should of known. Just like my brothers and sister after their music practice. So I said to myself I'm going to double my efforts. So after every track practice I ran all the way home three miles (Non Stop). And when I was running through Town some people we're whistling at me. So I trained real hard that spring and at the end of my track season, I was running the half mile in two minutes twelve seconds and running the mile in five minutes flat.

That summer of 1979, I worked at the restaurant again doing dishes, etc. with my friend Mark. I rode my bike back and forth again to work for a fourteen-mile round trip. When I rode my bike, I would ride on the edge of the road on the white line but people with cars would see you and push you right off on the dirt. I never understood that! I guess people on bikes weren't nice to car drivers. So that summer when I was doing other things in town, I decided to park the bike and run where ever I was going.

One day, I was really excited and decided to run a ten mile round trip to buy a new Bible when I was seventeen years old. I was thinking about when my parents bought my sister Jenny a Bible on her sixteenth birthday. So I decided to buy the Living Version Bible because the King James Version was too hard to understand. So on my way home, I had a little smile on my face, saying to myself, "Now I have my own Bible, too!" I began to think of Ephesians 6:16, *"In every battle you need faith as your shield to stop the fiery arrows aimed at you by Satan. And you need the helmet of salvation and the sword of the spirit-which is the Word of God."* So I'm thinking when we have people that are mean to us with their words and tear us apart; I have my weapon of choice, I have my sword and shield. That's the power in this Bible which is knowledge from God—the book of truth!

I loved to read my new Bible and one day, I was reading upstairs in my bedroom. I came across a verse that means a lot to me so I highlighted it in my Bible. 1 Corinthians 9:24-27: *"In a race, everyone runs but only one person gets first prize. So run your race to win. To win the contest, you must deny yourselves many things that would keep you from doing your best. An athlete goes to all this trouble just to win a blue ribbon or a silver cup. But do it for a heavenly reward that never disappears. So run straight to the goal with purpose in every step. I fight to win. I'm not just shadowboxing or playing around. Like an athlete, I punish my body, treating it roughly, training it to do what it should, not what it wants to. Otherwise, I fear that after enlisting others for the race, I might be declared unfit and ordered to stand aside."* Yes, that's true; we must train hard to be the best.

Fall was here and it was time for back to school. It's my eleventh grade year, and I just joined the junior varsity team in cross-country (three mile races). I was never the best runner there, but I ran a little varsity sometimes. I've noticed some kids that are the best would have a big head and they wouldn't even give you the time of day! They would keep you down and their attitude would show their disregards toward others. The way they carried themselves, arrogant and prideful … I was looking for this verse in my Bible, Proverbs 16:18: *"Pride goes before destruction and haughtiness before a fall."* I'm thinking of that guy that is so great in cross-country. I told myself, "I never want to be that way."

Well, kids can be so cruel. The regular kids were making fun of me. I was walking to my Special Ed classes. Now I'm thinking, "Didn't they just degrade themselves? Here,

they're smarter than me. Now who is the intelligent ones?"
Then that spring was track season and they had to have two
captains again. I wasn't the last one picked this time! But I
saw the pain on this one guy being the last one still on the
bench. This really bothered me and if it was going to continue, I was ready to say something but then they picked
him. I remember when they had basketball, volleyball, or
tag ball, I would be the last one picked and still sitting so I
know how it feels. That spring I ran track, I wasn't the best
but I was the third fastest on my team. I was finally on the
first year varsity.

I ran a 4:42 mile and a 2:06 half mile in my junior year
in school and the leader guy kept me down and wasn't nice
to me. He didn't respect me. I vowed that the next year I
would be the best runner on my team, and I'm not letting
anybody stop me no matter what! I'm going to give it my
all. I have to! And I'm never going to be stuck up! Oh dear
Lord, I want to be nice to everybody. I'm going to be the
best and I'm running for you, Jesus. This summer I'm taking the year off work and I'm going to train, train, train, all
summer long. I'm going for the school record in the mile,
and I'm going to show everybody. I'm going to be nice to
everyone and show respect too. At the end of my junior
year, I won the Most Improved trophy on my track team
for the mile! I had taken two minutes off my time!

It was June of 1980. School was out, and all summer,
I'm running 60 to 80 miles a week with Sundays off. I
ran in my neighborhood with my stopwatch that I bought
myself. I measured the ten blocks for my mile run. My
mom sometimes rode her bike with me. I also ran a lot of
long distance up the hill on Randolph Street, up through

the woods with hills. I never wore ear phones when I was running. I wanted to listen to real nature. The birds in the sky and thinking of the Lord. Also I was motivated every morning before I started running I would listen to certain song's at home like E.L.O. Living Thing, Telephone Line, Strange Magic and of course my favorite Mr. Blue Sky. I made it a habit to run fast uphill when I came to one. I figured it would give me an edge over others because I noticed others would slow down on the big hills, plus pick up my pace running faster up hills which helped me for training for my mile run in track! So then, I would run out to Cedar Run Road on out to the country-running fifteen miles non-stop. I never rode my bike at all. I ran in town, whatever I was doing. I trained real hard that summer.

Fall was coming and it was time for my last year of school. I had Driver's Ed class my senior year. The beginning of the semester, I passed the driver's training but failed the written test. So I wasn't getting my driver's license that year. That didn't make me feel good at all.

Well, I was on the cross-country team and I was the strongest trainer there. But it seemed any time we raced, I was behind the whole team. I failed to realize I didn't have the correct shoes on. I was racing with my trainer shoes and everybody else was wearing their lightweight running shoes. Toward the end of the season, I got smarter, I bought some lightweight running shoes and then I was keeping up with the other racers.

My mind didn't feel right anyway. What about cross-country? I was thinking a lot about my mile run in track. We got second place in regionals on our cross-country team and we qualified for the State Meet at Brookwood in Battle Creek. The races were three miles and my best time was just under sixteen minutes, 15:55. There were seven on our varsity team. We didn't win, but at least we qualified for the state meet.

I remember sometimes before we raced, we would get a motel for the night, and about two in the morning, I would get up and go for a walk outside. I liked looking at the stars and enjoyed the peacefulness and quietness. Then I could talk to the Lord by myself. After that, I would go back in to the motel.

Our cross-country season was over in November. During my second semester, I had a class I really liked—Graphic Arts. I was thinking what I was going to do for a career when I got out of school. I had to memorize the California type set! And I learned how to run the offset presses and set them up plus put the pads on the rollers. It was one of my regular classes. My teacher gave me an *A*. I also had to have Government Class and I had to pass in order to graduate from school. I was doing very badly and I needed a tutor. I had lots of studying and lots of headaches oh all these disruptions in our life that we are required to do.

In 1980, they changed the yards to meters ... our track season was starting in March 1981. Our assistant coach for distance runners asked us to turn in a paper on which we wrote our goals for the half mile, mile or two-mile for the season. I don't remember what I wrote for the mile but when he looked at my paper, he said out loud in front of everybody, "Did you see this, Karl said he's going to run the half mile in 1.59 One fifty-nine." He said, "Come on, no way!" I didn't say anything, but I felt bad. A couple guys from track had a smirk on their faces and I said to myself

I'm going to show them and the assistant coach too! I feel it's all I have to show and I'm not letting anyone beat me because all these other kids are smarter than me! And I'm not! So I'm staying at my peak performance but I'm also going to be nice to everybody no matter what.

There was one guy on the track team that kept bothering me. I felt uncomfortable many times going to practice but I'm not letting him stop me from going. Sometimes, it would be raining and they cancelled track practice. Then we would play basketball in the gym. I was terrible at it as I couldn't dribble or even make a basket. They would laugh at me. So I didn't play anymore. The next time, I would walk around the gym or go outside to run in the rain by myself. One day, I saw Tom feeling really bad and he was up on the second or third row sitting on the bleacher in the gym. I went up to him and asked if he was all right. He said, "Why would you care? I'm mean to you." I told him that doesn't matter how you treat me. I sat down next to him and said, "The Lord loves you, Tom. Do you know that?" I hope to this day, he remembers that and will never forget it. Nothing else was said and I didn't ask. I've always felt deep within my heart that I always wanted to please others but it took me years to find this love within myself. But my love for others is still always greater!

Now I'm thinking to myself, why am I the best track runner in the 1600 meters my senior year and I remember when others were the best in their senior year. They would be mean to me. Now I'm the best and I want to be nice to others and others that aren't as good as me want to treat me badly? What a reversal! My parents taught me that no one is better than anyone else. They taught me respect toward others and manners. I remember at one race, one of my teammates said his dad is here to see him win the mile run, and I'm thinking to myself, "My dad's not even here to watch me run so your dad's going to watch you lose to me." I was kind of ticked! Forgive me Lord. I just need this! When we had a track meet I always kept the Lord close to my heart. Also I played this one song in the morning at home on my eight track player and I memorize my theme song All Day for my mile run on Race Day! It was electric light orchestra – Mr blue sky it made me feel powerful and I lead the whole race out of 50 runners to finish First Place that day!

In another race, the thoughts went through my mind—I ran the 1600 meters in 4.36 and I have to at least run in the low 4.30 so I can stay ahead of the competition. This was because I felt really badly because I led the whole four laps until the last second in the mile. I was kind of gliding in for the finish line because I was tired. By then, I felt the pull of the tape and I didn't know until it was too late. That's when we hosted Muskegon Mona Shores that day and the two of us had our track picture on the front page of the newspaper in the Sports section. Then the next week, we had a track meet with the Muskegon Red's. I asked the Lord to speed up my time and I won first place with a time of 4.31.5 personal best. My head coach was real happy with that and so was I. I broke the course school record that day. In another race, some of these kids from down state were running 4.22 in the 1600 meters. I didn't realize these kids were so fast. WOW! The big regionals! Then one day, I remember my assistant coach came up to me and said, "If you had brains, you would be dangerous."

Actually', I was thinking where did that come from? Now I'm really feeling bad. Why would he say that? Aren't you the one teaching me this?

Then one day, we were at the LMAC track meet in Benton Harbor—the big one! Now I not only thought about what my assistant coach had said earlier that I couldn't run the 800 meters in 1.59 but I also felt bad because we lost our best 800-meter runner because he had shin splints. He was very fast and ran a 1.59 flat in the 800 meters in his junior year. Now our head coach needed someone for that race. So I'm praying to myself all the way down there on the school bus, help me Lord, to run the 800 meters in 1.59. I believe I can do it. So that day, I ran 1.59 in the 800 meters and 4.31 in the 1600 meters. I got fourth and third place in the 1600 meters that day. My head coach ran up to me, with his stopwatch, all excited and said, "Karl, do you know you ran the 800 meters in 1.59?" I got two medals that day! I felt kind of bad because I didn't win, but he reassured me I was all right!

When we ever felt down after our track meet was over and we were headed home on the school bus, I remember our head track coach, "Lober," would always say on the school bus, "I don't care if you didn't get first place. What I want to know is that you gave it your 100%. And I'm happy about that! That's all I want to hear. Great Job! Well done!" Our track head coach was really nice with kids and

he is one of my favorite people. He is the best—Coach

John P. Lober!

One day, we got off the bus for a track meet at Petoskey and I noticed a trophy on their table. It was a special event for the Cliff Buckmaster for the mile. I thought how badly I felt for not making the top three in the big regional event! I ran the 1600 meters in 4:31 again and didn't make the top three to compete in the state meet. So it's my senior year and I'm not going to state meet! I felt this trophy was for me. I had worked really hard for this for three years. I'm saying, Lord, I want to win this one for my dad. When we were ready to race, there must have been thirty runners there and I ran hard and lead the whole race to finish first. Then they had another heat with another thirty runners and I'm thinking all I have to worry about is someone betting my time! Well, no one touched my time. When I got home, I waited for my dad to get home from work, I told him, "Look what I won!" I was all excited … I didn't get the right reaction from him. He was overstressed from work and tired.

I simply thought him seeing my trophy that he would come to my next track meet. I went upstairs in my bedroom. Feeling kinda down … Placed my medal that the four of us won for the 4x4 mile relay that day and my trophy for my mile run with my other trophy and medals on my table and thought to myself. I guess I did this for my own accomplishment.

I said to myself, this is it! My last track meet … I was rated No. 1 out of the top ten in the honor roll meet in Northern Michigan. I was leading the whole race in the 1600 meters until the last curve of the race. A guy from another school passed me and ran a 4.28 in the 1,600 meters. So I got second place. Wow! Once in a while, I'll see my head track coach at certain events through the years he'll remind people what I did that day when I ran the 800 meters in 1:59. He never forgot that! Thank you, Coach Lober! I did that for you!

I remember through my track races, I went home and complained to my mom about my dad not watching me at my track races. My mom said, "I don't want you talking bad about your dad! He's a very hard worker and he supports this whole family. He never drinks and he always comes straight home after work. He never calls in sick and your dad is a very good man." My mom was right. Our dad has been so busy he hardly has time with my events and my brother's and sister's music concerts. But he is a great father at home… he was very tired from all the hard working days. Some days, he would work fourteen hours.

At the end of our track season, we have a banquet with award ceremony's and some of the staff member's made me a purple heart award out of paper. I was running against an all natural athlete. He runs the 1600 meters in 4:14 and I overheard his coach say just before the race to run in the low 4:30's because he's running other events. So I'm thinking all I have to do is hang right behind him and my last lap I'll give it my all. I just ran the first lap in sixty seconds. Turning the curve, holding second in a strong field of thirty runners in a Clare invitational track meet when suddenly misfortune struck.

Some guy behind me stepped on my calf muscle with his cleats and fell on top of me. I didn't want to quit! And forced myself up. My leg was bleeding but I still finished the race with a time of 4:45 in the 1600 meters. Seventeen seconds behind the winner.

CHAPTER 5

Welcome to Adulthood

June 11, 1981, was graduation day. We had about 980 in our class, and it took me forever to graduate because my last name was Olson. They went alphabetically from A to Z. On graduation day, our parents wanted all of us kids to not throw our hats so they could take our pictures at home.

I heard some of the grads say it's time for house parties; that's not for me. I went home with my parents and they had a nice cake and ice cream celebration. They took my picture with my track trophies and metals. I had a nice quiet time and then went to bed for the night.

Later the next day, I thought about what am I going to do with my life. The first thing was getting my driver's license at the Secretary of State office because I failed in the beginning of my senior year in school. So I went down there and passed the written test.

My dad had a little talk with me and said, "Now that you have graduated, you are an adult!" He also said, "Now is not the time for vacation but to get busy. Get a job and work." I knew he meant pay rent. He didn't have to tell me. I already knew. So I went all over town filling out applications for work that summer. One of those places was a pie factory. I know if you want a job, you have to keep bothering them so you let them know you're interested. This job was above minimum wage too!

Mark, my good neighbor, asked if I wanted a restaurant job doing dishes again. I reluctantly said yes. So I filled out an application at a different restaurant where he currently worked. It wasn't always a lot of fun working there. The head chef would keep you busy doing prep cooking for the banquets and at the end of the night at 11:00 p.m., he would leave you. There you were way behind with three big sinks full of pots and pans, dishes piled high at your dishwasher station. You would be there until 4:00 a.m. It all had to be done or you would be written up. This happened all the time. This was a big restaurant.

My dad always told me to be a good worker and do what you're told. If they ask you to come in on your day off, you tell them "Yes" so you look good in their eyes. Now I did that a lot of times.

I had some money saved up for a car and I wanted to buy a new car like the other kids when they got out of school. My dad told me, "No you're not! You can find a used one in the newspaper and I'll help you." I told him, "I want a new one at the car lot." My dad said if you do, "I'll double your rent." I asked him, "Why are you doing this to me?" He said, "Because you need to learn to be responsible.

You don't just go on a whim and buy whatever you want. You need to budget your money."

He also taught us other key principles like credit card debt. When you charge that card up, you need to pay it off within thirty days. Never pay monthly payments on cards. If you don't have enough money to cover that card in your bank, you don't do it!

Meanwhile at the restaurant, I continued to work there for a year. I asked the manager if I could have a raise. He looked right at me and said, "No, because you have an attitude problem." I looked at him and said, "I'm not the one with the attitude." Well he said, "No, that's it! I'm done talking." I'm thinking of all I do in here, I bust my back and they treat me like this! One day, the head chef told me, "Karl, no matter where you go, you're going to have someone like me give you a bad time." He said a bad word, and I don't want to repeat it. I felt really bad when he said it.

I had lots of bad days in there. One day, I told my dad how they were treating me. I said, "I'm going to quit." My dad said, "No, you're not! The boss may not always be right but he is the boss! You can quit if you want to but make sure you have another job lined up first. Then you can quit. Otherwise, do not quit! Get in there, Go, I love you!"

I went out searching for a different job. I went back to the pie plant to fill out another application and bothered them a lot. There was no response from them so I decided to go to TBA for vocational training in graphic arts press printing. I remember in school I was pretty good at running the offset press machine. So after I got more training, I went out to different press shops. I filled out applications and got an interview. The boss said he had to hire a family guy over me because he has a wife and kids and you don't. I thought, isn't that discrimination! Then the next interviewer at another shop said, "I got this one guy who can fix them as well as run them, can you?" That wasn't me.

Meanwhile I'm still working at the restaurant. I had to work a lot of holidays and even Sundays which I didn't want to do. I had to work Christmas Day 1982. I was carrying a five-gallon bucket of scalding water. As I was walking, I slipped on the floor where there was water on the floor. I slipped backwards with all the water splashing on my face, chest, and arms. Everybody rushed me out the backdoor into a snowbank. My chest was okay because I was covered with an apron.

One of the waitresses drove me to the emergency room. I had second-degree burns on my upper shoulder and on some of my neck, third-degree burns on my underarms and first-degree on my face. My face was all red but I was lucky. The Lord must have been watching me! They put all this white lotion all over me. My parents came up to see me and that night I went home with them. I just didn't understand this at all. Here I've been drilled about cleaning up the floor many times, and here it happened to me. Someone left water on the floor. Why? Why didn't they clean it up?

I had the rest of the week off and went back to work after New Year's. I worked lots of hours all through the summer, volunteered to work on my days off when they needed someone because they had dishwashers that quit. I told my dad, "I'm sick of working, can I quit? They are making me do too much!" My dad said no. I said, "But I'm the youngest in this family." My dad said, "That's a cop-out, not in this family." I told him, "But I have A-D-D." My dad said, "I don't want to hear it. You're going to be treated just like everybody else." I guess I wanted to be pampered. But then there's a part of me that I felt I wanted this sense of accomplishment for my own hard work.

One day, they called me and wanted me to come in and I told the boss, "Sorry, I have plans today." He said, "Fine, if you can't be there for us, we won't be there for you!" I was kind of ticked so I said, "Fine." and hung up the phone. I went in Monday morning and my time card was gone. So I went to the main office to talk to the General Foreman. She didn't help me at all. She just said, "That's right." I thought of all the times where I went in to work on my days off.

So after that, I went down to file for unemployment. I waited for a couple weeks and nothing happened. Finally, I called the unemployment office and asked what was wrong. They told me that I had been fired. I agreed with them but requested an appointment to speak with someone. On my way to the appointment, I prayed for God to help me. The man told me I was fired. I said, "Yes, because I didn't want to come in on my day off." So that was it, he stamped my papers and said, "OK." I received my unemployment check plus back pay. I breathed a fast "Thank you, Lord" prayer.

CHAPTER 6

Dealing with Significant Loses in Your Life

I ran over to see my grandma who lived behind my parent's home. She had a problem when her toe became blue. She had diabetes. My parents took her to the hospital and they were able to save her toe. But she had other problems so they kept her at the hospital for now.

While I was unemployed, I was really trying to get into the pie factory plant. I'd been trying for three years at this point. I was nervous because I knew I had to get a job fast. My dad was on my heels. Finally, I decided to call my Special Ed teacher and she helped me get in. Someone she knew in the plant who was high up owed her a favor. So she finally got me in that December, 1983. l was so excited because I would be making double the pay that l was making at the restaurant. I said to myself, "I worked at the restaurant for two years, two months, too long!"

On Christmas Day, Grandma came home from the hospital for just the day. She went back after we had our dinner that evening. A week after New Years of 1984 she died. I didn't realize she was that bad. I really had a hard time and couldn't get over her death. Every morning, I got up, I couldn't stop feeling bad; every day for about three weeks, my mom had a hard time with my depression.

One night, I had a dream. It was so big and like reality. Was that a dream? Grandma came down from heaven and her face was full of smiles. She said, "Don't cry for me, Karl. I can have anything I want even my candy!" Her face, I never forgot it, so full of smiles! And as she was leaving, I was feeling bad again. She was at a distance away and I saw her back. She turned right around and said, "Now stop crying, I'm living a great life! OK, Karl?" The next morning, I ran down stairs and told my mom about the dream. She noticed I was happy every day after that. I will never forget that dream!

I can remember all the fun I had with my grandma. I loved her so much. During the late seventies to early eighties, I went over there to watch *Love Boat, Quincy and Fantasy Island* with her. She always had candy over there and she liked to share.

When I worked in the pie factory, I didn't realize how rough it was working there. You had to be an industrial worker and be willing to work demanding hours—fifty to sixty hours a week, six days per week. Some of the people were not very pleasant to work with. I remember doing a specific job and the group leader was sitting at his desk when the supervisor would come in, too. They would tell me to do these other jobs as well and when someone else was doing a different job on our line. They sometimes would call in sick. So they would make me do his job, plus doing other jobs as well which he didn't have to do. And that person doing my job didn't have to do anything else except that one specific job! I've seen this happen to me a lot of times. And the supervisor would be sitting with the group leader at his table quietly laughing at me.

I'm thinking life isn't fair! Why is it certain people get away with stuff and others don't? My dad told me to keep my mouth quiet and do what I was told. I always do, and they make me do extra. They know I'm a really hard worker! Maybe that's why? My Special Ed teacher told me in junior high school a long time ago that I was going to have a hard time as I grew up because I looked just like a normal guy but having a learning disability and seeing you are slow, they will bother you. They may not understand this. So I explained this to my supervisor many times and some people can take advantage of you because of this and have a low disregard of you but I am aware of what's going on and I have feelings.

It was spring of 1984 and I asked my dad if I could move into my grandma's house behind my parent's home. He said, "Yes." But my rent went up which I understood. One day, I came home from a hard day of work and watched a movie. It was about deep sea diving for gold on a sunken ship under water. They found gold bullion bars, lots of them. They started to pick them up but they were too heavy to bring up from the ocean floor. So they invented a basket with a rope to bring them up.

That night I had a dream that I was deep sea diving. I had two gold bullion bars in my hands. I was coming up from the ocean floor to the surface. Then I woke up and it was all gone. My hands were sweating, NO GOLD! I was thinking if I had one of those gold pieces, it would be worth about one hundred grand a piece.

Now, have you ever dreamed the same dream twice? Well, I did, and in this dream I knew I was dreaming, why, because I could see myself. I thought about this deeply, thinking AHA! Now if I could grab one gold piece, I would have one hundred grand and I could quit my job. This time I used both my hands and grabbed on to it tightly. I finally reached the top of the ocean surface again! And I awoke with my hands sweating. Empty! No gold!

Now in that dream, I learned something. God was telling me two things. *First* in that dream, I noticed how quickly it was over from beginning to end. God was telling me just like that dream that's how short this life is. The *second* thing that God was telling me was "don't worry about getting rich because just like that dream, that's how quickly it will be over." The Lord told me to just work hard and have a good life down here because life is fleeting!

As I gave this great thought and prayer, I opened the Bible to Psalms 73:20. *"This present life is only a dream! They will awaken to the truth as one awakens from a dream of things that never were."* Isn't that amazing? God showed me this, thank you, Lord.

At work they put me on a different line where I worked with a different group leader. This guy would swear at people on the line, throw pies in the ram can and put his hands on you. Then when you complained to your supervisor about him, they would do nothing. I said to myself am I back in grade school again? I have seen a lot of people quit, but I couldn't, no matter what. This went on every day. I told my dad about this and he said, "Just put in your years and keep your mouth closed. Someday you can retire!" I said, "People are mean to me and I'm scared too!" My dad said, "Let me tell you something. You'd better be scared of me more than that place because I'll tell you what, if you don't make it in there, I'll throw you out of that house you're living in and you can live somewhere else. Streets!"

I said to him, "Why are you doing this to me?" My dad said, "Because I want you to make it in this life. And when I'm dead and gone, I want you to be independent! On your own! I love you!"

I remember a long time ago my oldest brother, Paul, said in his early twenties, "Dad, I don't think you should do a job if you don't like your boss." Dad jumped off the couch and said, "Listen here, kid, who put the shoes on your feet, the roof over your head, and the clothes on your back, don't give me that!" The truth hurts but my dad was right. He always told me the one that stays on the job the longest, gets ahead.

November of 1984: Bad News! My grandma Beeman died. She had a little vacation home in Tampa, Florida, through the years and they had to fly her body back to Michigan where we had her funeral. This was my mom's mother. It was really sad but I was kind of prepared for it. I had already experienced this situation with my dad's mother. I felt more relaxed because I knew where she was going. Heaven! I missed her very much but I know she is living a better life than us. I have a lot of great memories of her. I loved spending time and talking with her. And I loved to hug her. Once in a while, our family went to see her for dinner and she made the best homemade biscuits. We did lots of swimming at her cottage on Duck Lake. Out back she had a big pond and we did a lot of fishing.

Sometimes, my mom would let me spend the night there and I did lots of fishing. I caught Bluegills, Sunfish and large-mouthed Bass, big ones! I remember the time we were there on Sunday. I went fishing which we weren't allowed to do on Sundays because Sunday is the day of rest for the Lord. My dad pulled me by the ear and told me I was grounded in the house—*now*. He's right.

I had other memories when I was little. I loved to play with my miniature yellow Tonka Trucks at her beach on Duck Lake. I had about four or five of them, my dad had a sandbox behind our house and I spent hours and hours out there. I also had a pet hamster that was in a habit trail that he ran all over in.

Anyway, back to work. There are certain times some of the coworkers are just mean to you on a daily basis and it's really hard going in there. It's like gritting your teeth. "Oh my, another day!" You say to yourself. I know what my dad would say, "Stay the course. If you were a rich man, you could quit but you're not!" I wanted to pay close attention to myself to see if it's me causing all this trouble. I need to understand why these people are so mean to me. Is it me? I really had to evaluate my life and see for myself if I was doing wrong to others. I finely came to a serious conclusion with myself and aware of what I was doing on a close observation with myself. I observed it's not me, it's them. Like my mom always told me, "You are not responsible for their anger." They have a problem. So I got down on my knees to pray for those who were persecuting me. It's hard to do but I must. Jesus tells us to love your enemies in Luke 6:27-33, *"Listen all of you, love your enemies. Do good to those who hate you. Pray for the happiness of those who curse you; implore God's blessing on those who hurt you. If someone slaps you on the cheek, let him slap the other too! If someone demands your coat, give him your shirt besides. Give what you have to anyone who asks you for it; and when things are taken away from you, don't worry about getting them back. Treat others as you want them to treat you. Do you think you deserve credit for merely loving those who love you? Even the godless do that! And if you do good—is that so wonderful? Even sinners do that much!"* Yes, yes, we need to love everybody! And pray for them because Jesus loves us.

CHAPTER 7

Four Life-Changing Miracles

This entire trauma caused me to get to the place where I experienced four miracles. It all happened in the spring of 1985 when the Lord opened it all to me.

First Miracle … What kind of man do you want me to be, Jesus? I just opened the Bible after praying for three hours.

Second Miracle … How do you want me to pray, Jesus? I thought about this and my eyes looked right at the answer.

Third Miracle … How can I serve you, Lord? I just opened the Bible again after praying an hour and he showed me.

Forth Miracle … I prayed another hour and I just opened the Bible again and God showed me.

Now this is how it all happened and what the Lord told me while I was having a really hard time.

It was the middle of the day on Saturday, the ninth day of February. My dad had chest pain and my mom drove him to the hospital. He spent a couple nights there while they were doing a bunch of tests. When we went up to see him, we waited and waited in the ward. Finally, the doctor came in and said he needed emergency surgery for a 90% heart blockage. This would require him to have a quadruple bypass surgery and they didn't have a heart surgeon here in Traverse City.

So they scheduled his surgery on Thursday, February 14, 1985. They rushed him up to Petoskey, Michigan, in an ambulance on that Monday morning to get him prepped for surgery. My sister went with Mom in her car following behind the ambulance. I stayed home in the little house and worked Monday through Wednesday. Thursday and Friday they closed the plant. I couldn't believe it because they never closed the plant. It's very unusual for them to close at all.

The Record-Eagle newspaper featured an article on the front page about Northwestern Michigan College breaking a record of closing the campus for three days— the first time in its thirty-year history. Well, we worked that Wednesday when a lot of other businesses were closed. That whole week kept me pretty busy. We had blowing and drifting snow. I kept bouncing back and forth from work and to shoveling snow every day. My parents lived on a corner city lot so there were extra sidewalks plus two driveways. I had to keep everything open for the mailman. The driveways kept getting plugged up when the snowplow went past which added snow that was a foot deep.

When they finally closed the plant on Thursday, I thought I was going to get a break where I could go up to Petoskey for my dad's surgery. But then the state police gave the notice on the news to stay off the roads unless for emergency purposes only. Otherwise, if you were caught on the roads they would arrest you—and I'm thinking, I knew it! We go through this every year. People are all over the roads getting stuck in their cars because they can't stay home. So the state police said if you needed emergency assistance, call them.

I stayed home for two days and thought I could keep my mind off my dad because I was so busy shoveling. I did all the walks and both driveways twice each day and I kept telling myself, *"I can do all things through Christ who strengthens me."* (Phil. 4:13). Then Saturday morning came and I was finishing up the snow shoveling plus what the plow pushed in. It took me awhile but I finally got it done. Then I drove to the bank to get some money. I looked at my receipt; I noticed I didn't have much left in the account. I was very upset with myself. I thought I had more money than that …

Needing groceries at home, I went to the grocery store, returned home to pack my clothes for a night in Petoskey, and I was so wound up. Getting up there with all the traffic; worked up; so upset; why is everything so hard these days.

It was Saturday when I arrived in Petoskey. I asked at the front desk when I arrived to get Dad's room number in the Intensive Care Unit. Up near Dad's room, a doctor stopped me in the hallway to say, "If you feel emotional at all, you need to leave because your dad doesn't need to be upset."

I went into his room but I wasn't prepared for what I saw! He looked in really bad shape—terrible. He was on a bed and looking straight up to the ceiling because he couldn't move his head and he had bruises all around his neck because there were IVs pinching his neck, so he was stiff from that. But the first thing I noticed was the tube they had down his throat so he couldn't talk. He had a hard time breathing and he seemed very uncomfortable.

He had metal staples from his stomach up to his chest and also all the way down his right leg, almost to his groin because they needed the artery from that leg so they could use it in his heart. There must have been two or three tubes in and out of his stomach and at least three drip bottles down his arm for IVs plus he was wearing a catheter bag too! He was also hooked up to a monitor that had four or five lines with all the beeping noises. He had bruises around different parts of his body. He was alert when I walked in there—and all this time, I must have been there not more than twenty seconds in the room. He couldn't move, and I was on the left side of his bed. So all he could do was turn his eyes my way. And then he looked right at me and I saw a tear drop down from his right eye. I never saw my dad do that! I bolted out of the room and I lost it! I went out in the hallway in shock and tried to contain myself but it was really hard. I froze up leaning next to the wall in a standing position while quietly whimpering … and tears were running down from my eyes and they saw how upset I was. I was trying to hide it and be strong like my dad but it was so unbearable. I couldn't even think any more. "Oh my, oh my," I was saying to myself, "oh no, oh no." Well after that, I don't know what happened. I seemed to have lost track of time. I guess it must have been evening. My mom came out into the hallway and said, "Come on, we're going out to Big Boy's to eat just up the hill from the hospital. We're going to meet Aunt Carrie there." Just the three of us. I didn't eat much at all and I was very quiet.

My mom said, "We're leaving our cars in the hospital parking lot for the night. We can go to her church in the morning and then we'll drop you off for your car so you can go home after that." I thought, and of course, go back to work. So after eating lunch, my mom and I went to Charlevoix in Aunt Carrie's Car to her home. Mom and my aunt were in the front seat and I was in the back seat by myself.

I didn't say anything because I had a lot on my mind. I was really stressed. When we arrived at her apartment, they got out of the car and went into the apartment. I stayed in the car and started crying really hard. I locked the door. About a half hour later, my mom wondered what had happened to me so she came out to the car. I wouldn't unlock the door and I wouldn't even talk. I kept feeling really bad and thinking my dad might die. I was feeling so, so alone. I don't even have a girlfriend. I was also thinking about my bank account. "When I get home on Monday, I need to get my check from work."

Mom kept talking to me. Finely I unlocked the door and we went into the apartment to go to bed since it was getting late. The next morning, we went to Aunt Carrie's church. While we were there, I kept thinking about getting my check on Monday. After church, we went out to eat and then drove up to Petoskey so I could get my car. Mom gave me a hug and she went back into the hospital to see my dad. I drove back down to Traverse City so I could go to work. I got home that Sunday evening, got something to eat, and set my alarm because I had to be at work at 1:00 a.m. on Monday.

When I went to work, I talked to the security guard first on my way in. I asked them for my check. He checked and said I didn't have one. I said, "What? Really? What's going on? Why don't I have a check?" He looked again and said, "No, I don't have a check for you." I asked him if they even made a check for me. The security guard said, "I don't know but maybe somebody else took your check by mistake." I figured that's it, either way it could be. I was getting a little upset. Then I said, "Do you even know if I got a check?" He replied, "No, because we don't have any record of that." I asked him if he would notify personnel to make me another check for that week. He said he would and then I went into the plant to work. It took a good long week for that check to come in and when it did, I cashed it.

The next week after all that, I got a call from the office while I was really busy with my job. I walked all the way to the office and was thinking what now? The union steward was in there with the personnel lady who is also the assistant manager. When I sat down she said, "We have a serious problem here." She pulled out two checks and put them on top of her desk. She said, "Are these both your signatures?" I looked at them and said, "Yes, but I don't remember cashing them." I explained that I had had a lot of trauma in my life. I had lost both my grandmas in 1984; my dad had a four bypass heart surgery just a couple weeks ago in Petoskey. And now I feel really bad about this check problem. I'm very sorry about this and asked if I could just pay it back.

The personnel lady said, "Well, I'll be back. I have to discuss the situation with others." She was gone for about ten minutes. I was talking to my union steward about this mess. I have never forgotten getting a check before. Finally, she returned and said, "We are going to suspend you for three days and you will not be going back to work today. You will be going home and we have an appointment for Saturday to come in to discuss the situation further." I told her, "What's the problem? I will pay back what I owe!" "Sorry," she said. "We have to go through channels. This meeting is over for now." So I went out in the parking lot to get my car and go home.

I'm thinking I can't believe this. I still don't remember getting my check. But I must have. Well, I'll wait until my dad gets home. He'll know what to do. Oh, I feel really bad. It was two days later before my dad came home. Now I need to go in my parent's home and tell him but I better wait until he gets settled in. After a while, I went in and told my parents all about what had happened. I told them about the appointment for Saturday. I'm hoping everything is all right. They both said just wait and see what they will do.

Saturday morning came and I went in for my appointment. When I went in, the assistant manager was already in the office by herself. I was pretty nervous because she didn't say a word to me and she just stared at me. So I told her again how sorry I was and that I would pay back the money. She still said nothing. Now I was getting nervous because I'm waiting for the union steward who is now ten minutes late. He finally came in and said he's sorry for being late. He was really busy on the line so he couldn't leave right away and then he had to go to his locker room to get his books. As he came in, he plopped his books on the table. It startled me. He sat down next to me.

Now the assistant manager finely spoke. She said, "Now, I want to say since you are such a good worker, we are going to give you a choice. Now we don't usually do this but we are going to do this for you. You can quit or you will be fired. You decide what you want to do. You talk about it with your union steward. I'm going to walk out of the office for a few minutes." Then the union steward said, "What do you want to do?" I said, "I already know what I want to do. I don't need one minute to think about it. She can fire me because I'm not admitting to my guilt that I did this deliberately. I can't believe I came to this appointment for this."

She returned and said, "What did you decide?" The union steward didn't say anything. So I looked right at her and said, "I guess you'll have to fire me because I'm not going to admit my guilt that I deliberately did this." I let her know that I couldn't believe I had come in for this. So she said, "I don't believe you, and you stole from us." I replied, "I can't believe you would think that way about me."

I told her I had a serious situation. I had to clean out my locker all the while thinking I couldn't believe it. I felt really bad about this whole mess so I cleaned out my locker, walked out of the plant, went to my car in the parking lot, and went home.

Thinking about the meeting, I thought to myself, "I'm proud of what I said because I was being true to myself." But at the same time, I was feeling very hurt because she now had given me a criminal record for theft at the plant which would possibly make it impossible to get a job anywhere. I still had to go home and tell my dad. "I still don't remember that check. But I must have had it because they were both cashed at my bank. This is March 8, and I lost my job!" So I went to my parent's home and told them what had happened. My dad said, "Don't worry about it. Let the union steward take care of it. We'll call the personnel office later and talk with them. Just let us handle this. Don't you call and bother them. OK!" So I went back to my little house behind my parent's home.

Our family doctor sent a letter to the company as well as the heart doctor in Petoskey who sent a letter to the pie factory explaining how tragic and traumatic these events had been. He said I should have seen a video before I had walked into my dad's room. It explained about what my dad was going through. But there hadn't been time because of the snowstorm and blizzard we had that week.

My Special Ed. teacher wrote the company, too, explaining how I was. The company wouldn't even listen.

My parents left messages on their phone and they would not return the calls.

The next three weeks, I had a mental meltdown. I called Third Level Crisis Center several times, and I was so depressed. I had to pay my rent soon and I know my dad told me to not worry about it right now. But I am. He taught me to be independent. I just felt so horrible and just can't believe this situation I'm in. Every day, I wake up to another morning and it's just the same thing—nothing! What happened? Why am I in this perdition (eternal drama, hell)? Help me, Lord Jesus! I take a shower morning and night and I don't know what to do. It must be the end of March and it's about 8:00 p.m.!

I went back to that lonely dark shower thinking deeply about what I'm going to do. I went back in the living room to watch TV. I just can't watch anymore. I don't care if there is a special show on or not. I have to turn that TV off and come to you, Jesus. Why did I let you go in my prayer life? I need to let all this go and give it to you. Oh, I'm in anguish, I'm in anguish. I'm pacing back and forth in the little living room in my grandma's house.

Then I went into the kitchen and stared into the bathroom doorway. I looked and looked. Lord, I was trying to compose myself looking into that little shower room. I can't handle this anymore. Why do I feel this terrible hurt in my soul? I'm feeling really bad and I'm ready to do something drastic. I have to give this all to you, Jesus! I can't stand this anymore. I feel you wouldn't want me to do this! I'm just talking to you, Jesus, in this dark shower room on the floor for two hours. And I just forced myself up!

Walking through the kitchen to the living room, I looked out my little window and just saw my parent's kitchen lights go out! I couldn't go in that house because I know how my dad is and he wouldn't be happy with me the way I am. He would be very upset. Oh, Lord, my whole body is shaking so much. My life is about to *end now!*

CHAPTER 8

The Big Awakening of the Truth

It was ten at night and I hurried to turn the lights and TV off. I got down on my knees in front of the couch in the living room. Oh, dear Lord Jesus, I come to you. I'm in my depth of despair. I can't handle it anymore. I'm scared and I'm feeling really, really sick, Lord. Both my grandmas passed away in 1984. My dad had a four bypass open heart surgery on February 14 in 1985 and is now recovering at home. I thought he was going to die and I still don't know. While he is recovering at home, I had to tell him I got fired from my job this March. My parents called about my job and tried to talk with them and they wouldn't even listen. That stressed him out and he had a mild heart attack. The doctor said he wouldn't have survived if it wasn't for his heart surgery. Oh, dear Lord, I feel the blame for this. I feel really bad. I can't walk over to their house and load my troubles on them anymore. They have enough on their plate. My mom feels really bad and my dad gets mad. My dad just handles it differently. I've called Third Level Crisis Center too many times and they can't do anything for me. I don't understand why I got fired from my job. I can't see waking up to another day. I have to settle this with you, Jesus, tonight. You are my only hope. I feel frozen and I can't call the personnel manager at my work place. I'm sure they wouldn't even listen to me anyway! My parents said they would handle it I feel so hopeless and lost ... I'm to the lowest point of my life. I just want to lay down here and die ... I don't understand why I have had such a hard life, Lord. I've always been a good steward for you, Jesus. All my years in school and my track days, I didn't go out to wild parties. I was straight and never acted cool and didn't swear.

They noticed I was different in school because I lived for you, Lord.

Oh, dear Lord, you know in my past prayers I've been praying for a soul mate. I feel so alone and hurt. I want to be loved as well as I love her. I thought on my sixteenth birthday on that special day I would get a kiss from a girl. That never happened and here I am still here, twenty-three years old and never really dated anyone yet. Some people at church are telling me to be a Barnabus for you, Jesus. O dear Lord Jesus. We all want to be loved and wanted. This world is so hurtful and mean. Why are people so mean to others? I know, dear Lord, because people's hearts aren't for you. I asked if you could give me that special bond with a woman. That's the best gift you can give a man. We can be of one heart and mind and have you in the center of our lives, Lord. I feel this is as close as I can get to you on this earth, Lord. Our thoughts are for you and to share with each other. I never have had that special closeness.

This world needs more love toward each other. It seems anytime I asked a girl out, there would be some guy telling me to leave her alone. He would say, "Leave her alone; this one's mine. Ask any other girl but not this one." She would soon find out that he was a fast talker and liar and he would hurt her feelings. Now she' won't go out with anyone at all. Why have I struggled with this? Is it true that good guys are always last? It all made my self-esteem feel really low so I had a hard time approaching a girl.

I don't have anybody else to go to. I'm scared and I've been feeling like ending my life. I just want to do it. I've been thinking of slitting my wrist in that shower and watch myself bleed to death. It seems so easy to do and I wouldn't make a mess for anyone. No one would care anyway. But I'm coming to you Jesus. Oh, Jesus, I'm crying for your mercy. Everything's going wrong in my life. Oh, my body doesn't stop shaking. I give up. I surrender all to you, Jesus. What kind of man do you want me to be? Yes, that's it. That's what I want to know.

Oh, Jesus, I come to you with all my heart and every fiber of my being … Oh, Lord, when I come to you, I come to the Father. When I love you, I love the Father. You said in your Word to come to me through the Father. Jesus, you said, "I am the way. I am on the right hand of God." So I'm coming to you. I know when I come to you the Father in heaven is happy because he wants us to come to you. I know the Father in heaven hears everything but he wants us to recognize you, Jesus. You are my Savior, Jesus. You are the Savior of the whole world. You died for all of us, Jesus. You shed great drops of blood for all of us … You love all of us!

Hear my prayers, Lord Jesus. Oh, dear Jesus, I come to you so sincerely. Oh Jesus, I ask if you could show me a sign in the Bible. Please tell me, Lord. "I'm lost" without you. If you could just tell me. What kind of a man do you want me to be? Then I would be happy inside because I know it has come from you. I promise whatever you tell me, I will take it to my grave and never forget it. I will write this down in my Bible permanently, dear Lord Jesus.

Please show me a sign in the Bible. Oh, my body doesn't stop shaking. Please rescue me from this dark cloud. My prayer life must be weak. I haven't prayed like this in a long time. Oh, I'm so sorry, Lord. Why is it that we don't come to you until we have problems? Oh, my eyes hurt so much from crying, Lord. They sting and are sore. Oh, I'm so scared but I have to believe you're going to show me something.

You are my only hope, Jesus! I believe in your name. I'm not going to just flip through any pages either. I'm going to just open the Bible with my eyes shut and the first thing I see I'm going to just look at it. I'll read it in your name what you want me to know. Use my hands and eyes in your name, Jesus, Amen.

I turned the lights on, I picked up the Bible, and then I said again with my eyes closed, "I believe in your name Jesus. I said use my hands and eyes and I said what kind of man do you want me to be, Jesus?" as soon as I just opened the Bible to First Timothy chapter 1 my hand pointed to verse 19 with my finger. I opened my eyes and read what it said. "*Cling tightly to your faith in Christ and always keep your conscience clear, doing what you know is right. For some people have disobeyed their conscience and have deliberately done what they knew was wrong. It isn't surprising that soon they lost their faith in Christ after defying God like that. Hymenaeus and Alexander are two examples of this. I had to give them over to Satan to punish them until they could learn not to bring shame to the name of Christ.*"

I looked at the clock and noticed it was 1:00 a.m. Right then, I just thought to myself, "Lord, I feel this deep inside me like you were always trying to tell me something." I noticed there were two parts to this. First it says *cling tightly to your faith in Christ*. I believe this means we are not only to pray to him in our daily lives but when we have problems in our lives, we talk to him daily and we're always thinking of him; whether I'm in my car going to work or doing other business around town or just walking around my subdivision on a nice sunny day. I say to myself, "Lord help me to be nice to others and please guide and direct me in your name." I think of the poem "Footprints in the Sand" where it says that he carries us in our rough times wherever we are. In Psalms 16:8-9 it says, *"I am always thinking of the Lord; and because he is so near, I never need to stumble or fall. Heart, body, and soul are filled with joy."* Isn't that wonderful! Even in our sleep He cares and watches over us.

Now the second part is this: always keep your conscience clear doing what you know is right.

I remember when I was about twelve, I didn't have much money when I went to the store and decided to steal two pieces of candy putting them in my coat pocket on a Monday afternoon. When I did this I felt his strong voice like a shock in the back of my head saying "NO, Karl!" It bothered me but I still did it. The second day was a Wednesday when I took a couple pieces of candy again. I still felt that voice in the back of my head but not as strongly. The third day was on a Friday. I didn't feel that voice anymore but I still felt guilty because I still knew I was wrong. Well, that day as I was ready to leave, the store keeper grabbed me by the back of my shoulder, pulled me back into the store. He said to me, "Kid, I knew you were doing this all the time." He walked me behind the counter, sat me on the stool, and said, "Tell me your parent's phone number."

Really worried, I said, "Please don't call my dad, call the police." Of course then I saw a smile on his face and he probably thought, oh boy, this is a good one. So he called and I was so scared and embarrassed because people were coming in and I sat there on the stool waiting for my dad. He finally came in and with a stern look on his face, told the store worker, "I'll take care of it." I saw the look on my dad's face—very disappointed. I'm thinking, oh boy, now I'm going to get it.

So I got into his GMC truck and he took me home telling me to go down into the basement. He told me from the top of the steps, "Now I want you to think about what you've done." I must have been down there about three hours and I was wondering what he was going to do. Then he called from the top of the stairs to come on up and he didn't say anything else. So I went up all the way to the stairs to my bedroom on the second floor. It was probably a couple months later that I got the nerve up and said in the living room to my dad, "Why didn't you punish me for stealing that candy at the store?" He looked at me a couple seconds and didn't say anything. Then he sternly said, "Because you knew you were wrong, guilty, and embarrassed. The look on your face showed it. I felt you were punished enough." He was so right ... I never did that again.

Now, there are three aspects of our conscience. First, my thoughts from this story: I feel if we continue to keep doing bad things in our life we can lose our conscience which comes from God (our inner voice) because he will leave and go elsewhere to someone who will listen. So I feel our conscience is very important. You see, we can get these bad thoughts from Satan. In Mark 7:20 it says, *"It is the thought life that pollutes." Evil thoughts of lust, theft, murder, adultery, deceit, lewdness, envy, slander and pride, etc.* Afterwards we get the feeling from God telling us NO. That's our conscience. Isaiah 30:21 says, *"And if you leave*

God's path and go astray, you will hear a voice behind you say, 'No, this is the way; walk here.'"

It should be a warning to us that we shouldn't take lightly: our conscience always comes right to wrong never wrong to right. It's a reminder to do *right*. Romans 2:13-14 says, *"For down in their hearts they know right from wrong. God's laws are written within them; their own conscience accuses them, or something excuses them."*

The second aspect is if we cross that line such as murder, we may not be able to forgive ourselves. Something that God wouldn't let us forget because it is a serious crime. That's how deep this can go with our conscience—it's a warning from God. So we not only forgive others but also forgive ourselves. I'm afraid if we can't forgive ourselves for what we have done, Jesus won't forgive us. So listen closely to your inner voice before you ever do something like that. The devil lies to us by telling us that you can get away with murder. What he doesn't tell you is that you have to live with your conscience every day. Thinking of what you have done ... Proverbs 20:27 tells us, *"A man's conscience is the Lord's searchlight exposing his hidden motives."* At the end of our life, we will be exposed to Christ. The price may be your own soul. So don't let the devil get a foothold on you ... or it will be too late for you.

You see if we ever do a crime like this and know we are guilty and we are walking free on this earth! (We are not truely free) We are still a prisioner in our own mind!!

For we can not forget this horrible deed we have done.

We must turn ourself in to the authorities and then forgiveness will start in our live's we must have deep remorse and penitence then the Lord will forgive us. I also felt this third aspect about our conscience is Jesus was warning me not to commit suicide. Remember; always keep your conscience clear doing what you know is right. *"Haven't you yet learned that your body is the home of the Holy Spirit God gave you? And that he lives within you? Your body doesn't belong to you. For God has bought you with a great price. So use every part of your body to give glory back to God because he owns you!"* (I cor. 6: 19-20). So you see God didn't make any junk! We shouldn't throw ourselves away! "Thank you, Lord, for showing me this. It will stick with me the rest of my life. Hopefully, this opens a new door in your own heart and gives you a new perspective in your life. So listen to your conscience. It is our gift from the Lord. *Because of this, I try with all my strength to always maintain a clear conscience before God and man."* (Acts 24:16)

When I was thinking about my first miracle all of a sudden I thought to myself "How do you want me to pray, Jesus? My eyes looked down on 1 Timothy 2 and my hand moved down on verse eight. Just the second I thought about this, I see this, *"So I want men everywhere to pray with Holy hands lifted up to God free from sin, anger and resentment."*

Wow ... that was fast! Isn't that so true. How we live and how we act with love for others is how we should be week-to-week, month-to-month and year-to-year. Why do we always go back to sinning every week and asking for forgiveness? Jesus doesn't want that. Why can't we really stop ... and live for Jesus.

He wants us to come to him with our hearts pure to him free from sin in our daily life. That's what Jesus wants! In John 8:3-11, *we see where the Pharisees brought a woman caught in adultery and brought her in front of a staring crowd. They asked Jesus what they should do with her because Moses's law said to kill her. Jesus was sitting on the ground and stood up to say, "He who is without sin cast the first stone. So they all walked away one by one. Then he stooped down again and wrote in the dust."*

Jesus was left alone with just the woman. He stood again and said to her, "Where are your accusers? Didn't even one of them condemn you?" "No, Sir," she said and Jesus said, "Neither do I. Go and sin no more." Notice Jesus told her to go and sin no more. Why do we as Christians think it's OK to keep on sinning and asking God for forgiveness. You see, I have noticed some people call themselves Christians and still seek their own sin pleasure and aren't very nice to people.

"For when we are Christians, we are free from sin and it's power over us. So let's look at our old sin nature as dead and unresponsive to sin and instead let's be alive and do all things good for Christ and alert to him." (Rom. 6:7-11) Now I know in Ephesian 2:8-9 *For by Grace are ye saved through Faith and that not of yourselves. It is the Gift of God not of works least any man should boast.* Did we catch this verse. Now that we are Christian we are saved through Faith. And faith in God means obeying him and living right and with this free gift comes responsibility for this new life we live. By telling others of his word. And helping others. For it says in Roman 12:1-2 *we need to give our bodies to God as a living sacrifice, Holy the kind he can accept for what he has done for us. Is that too much to ask? Don't copy the behavior and customs of this world, but be a new and different person with a fresh newness in all you do and think.* (Yes we need to have a change of heart deep in our love for Jesus and others) Yes it says in James 2:14-17 *what's the use of saying we have faith and are Christians and we aren't proving it by helping others? Will that kind of Faith saved anyone? If you have a friend who is in need of food and clothing, and you say to him, "well, good-bye and God bless you; stay warm and eat hearty," and don't give him clothes or food, what good does that do? So you see, it isn't enough just to have faith. You must*

also do good to prove that you have it, faith doesn't show itself by good works is no faith at all—it is dead and useless. Also, in James 2:24, it says, "*So you see a man is saved by what he does, as well as what he believes.*" So we as Christians need to do good to others as well as believe.

There is an important verse in the Bible that really touches my heart in 2 Corinthians 6:3: "*We try to live in such a way that no one will ever be offended or kept back from finding the Lord by the way we act. So that no one can find fault with us and blame it on the Lord. In fact, in everything we do we try to show that we are true ministers of God.*"

Oh, isn't that so true … that's how we should be. I was so excited. I just felt so good inside. I want to give praise to you, Jesus.

I hurried up and turned the lights off in my little living room again behind my parent's home. I got down on my knees and thanked the Lord for the two miracles he had showed me. During the next hour, I felt this great spark inside me and his wonderful grace that came over me. I was so happy. I said, "How can I serve you, Lord, please tell me." I believe in your name, Jesus. I am so overwhelmed in my prayers to you, Jesus. I felt so good inside my heart.

I'm not going to just flip through the pages either. I'm going to just open the Bible like before and I'm going to point right at it with my fingers. The first thing I see, I'm going to just look right at it and read it in your name, Jesus. I believe you will show me an answer to my question because you would want me to know and your love is so great!

So after I prayed a whole hour, I opened my eyes, turned the lights on and said, "Use my hands and my eyes and show me what I can do for you. I believe in your name, Jesus." I said it again, "How can I serve you, Lord?" With my eyes closed, I just opened the Bible to the Book of Isaiah 12 and pointed my finger at verse 4. Opening my eyes the verse said, *"In that wonderful day, you will say thank the Lord! Praise His name! Tell the world about his wondrous love. How mighty he is! Sing to the Lord. For he has done wonderful things. Make known his praise around the world."*

I was so excited again. Oh Lord, You give me joy... thank you, Jesus...wow...wonderful joy fills my heart... I'm just filled! with your Holy Spirit and love ... I'm so overwhelmed ... tell everyone how mighty he is ... Jesus, our Lord. He loves us so much! He loves everybody in the whole world! I remember in my track days when I won a lot of the races, not all of them, but when I did I wanted to give praise to God ... in public but no one asked me. I wanted to say all my efforts are because of Jesus!

Now I'm thinking what is the proper way of serving Jesus? Jesus was showing his disciples how to do this. In John 13:15 how to follow his example by washing their feet so we can learn how to be a blessing to others. Yes you see, this is for all of us! Not just pastors in church we need to be a witness for others and think of others before ourself by being very humble, and not think as ourself so highly! It felt like I was down in the valley and I just walked on top of the mountain and met God ... like Moses did in the burning bush. Jesus Christ is wonderful. He is our channel in our prayers.

I want to tell you right now how he can do mighty miracles in our lives if we just let him into our lives.

I kept reading this verse Isaiah 12:4 and thinking how wonderful Christ showed me this for about twenty minutes. All of a sudden, I was in this great moment and something hit me hard. It felt like a dark cloud of doubt just came over me! I panicked and fell to my knees while quickly turning off the lights! I prayed for another hour.

Oh dear, Lord, why am I feeling this way? I have this terrible, terrible feeling. I feel like a black cloud just came over me and surrounded me. Oh my heart is aching; I don't want these bad feelings. Why am I feeling so, so bad? All of a sudden I have this sense of hopelessness. Please forgive me, Lord. Satan must be bothering me and I'm not going to let him win! JESUS! Why do I have this feeling like I want to throw this Bible in the closet? And forget it?

I'm not going to end it this way! I command you, Satan, to get behind me in the name of Jesus Christ! Oh Lord, he must flee because you said in your Word. I believe he must leave.

Oh dear Lord Jesus, when I come to you I come to the Father in heaven as well. You said come to me through the Father and I'm coming to you, Jesus. You are the reason for my three miracles, I know you are, I must believe. Oh, dear

Lord I'm hanging on the edge of the cliff and I'm falling. I see a rope and I must grab it. I'm hanging on the end of the rope. I must hang in there, oh please, help me! Lord Jesus, help me! My faith is very weak. This dark cloud is not going away. I pray in your name, Jesus. Get behind me, Satan! Oh my eyes are red like before from crying so much. I come to you.

Why would you listen to me? There are billions of people in the world doing their own things and here I am praying to you. I think of all the animals in the world and even the billions of insects that you watch too. So why would you bother with me. But I know you see the whole world! Going on and yet you *still* see me! And you wouldn't let me go because I'm here in your name, praying to you, Jesus. You even watch the ants in the whole world: many different kinds, billions and billions of them! More than the people in the world, it's going on now, Lord, even as I speak. You have everything in your order, Lord. Everything is in special order and a special way!

Oh, Lord, I'm down on my knees and I'm in anguish. Is this true? Is it real? Is this true? Is this a coincidence? Is there really a God? Forgive me, Lord. I'm so sorry for asking or thinking that. I have to believe these three miracles are from you. I promise when I open my eyes and turn on the lights again all in your name whatever you tell me in the Bible and when I open it again, I will listen and I will never forget it. I will let it penetrate my brain forever and write it down in my Bible. I'm asking this last question and I will be happy if you show me this miracle. Now I'm not going to just flip through any pages either just like the last time. The first thing I see when I just open the Bible and I open my eyes, please use my hands and eyes, Lord, Amen.

So after I prayed an hour, I turned the lights on then closed my eyes and said, "I believe in your name Jesus. Is this really true? Is there really a God? Oh, I'm sorry for asking this." As soon as I opened the Bible to the Book of Psalms 14 and pointed my finger at verse one, I opened my eyes. It said, *"That man is a fool who says to himself, 'There is no God!' Anyone who talks like that is warped and evil and cannot really be a good person at all. The Lord looks down from heaven on all mankind to see if there are any who are wise, who want to please God. But no, all have strayed away; all are rotten with sin, not one is good, not one! They eat my people like bread and wouldn't think of praying! Don't they know any better?"*

After I was reading this, I just looked up at the clock and noticed it was 4:00 a.m. I was very tired. I said, "Oh, Lord, I am very ashamed of myself. But I'm very glad also for telling me the answer to my question!" With that, I went to bed. My thoughts were still on this how he had just lifted me up! WOW! Oh, the Lord is just so wonderful. He opened up and showed me how mighty he is! I noticed how weak my faith was when I asked him this second time, "Is there really a God?" It seems as long as you trust with all your whole heart, He will come through for you, even when my faith broke down. 2 Corinthians 12:10 tells me,

"Since I know it is all for Christ's good I am quite happy about the thorn." And about insults and hardships, persecutions and difficulties; for when I am weak, then I am strong—the less I have, the more I depend on him, Jesus Christ. I just want to say that I am not ashamed for all my hardships in this life

because Jesus showed me the real purpose!

And I want to say reading the Bible and spending time in prayer are important! When I prayed and asked in Jesus's name for help, he showed me in the Bible. Because I believe in him that's why I pray to you, Lord. You really showed me. Thank you, Lord, for showing me these four miracles … Oh, I won't ever forget it … I wrote these down in my Bible! He will pick us up when we fall. Amen! All we need to do is ask. Then believe in him! *Jesus*!

Jesus used this illustration about our prayers—suppose you went to a friend's house at midnight, wanting to borrow three loaves of bread. You would shout up to him, "A friend of mine has just arrived for a visit and we have nothing to give him to eat." He would call down from his bedroom, "Please don't ask me to get up. The door is locked for the night and we are all in bed. I just can't help you this time: but I'll tell you this— though he won't do it as a friend, if you keep knocking long enough, he will get up and give you everything you want—just because of your persistence. And so it is in prayer—keep on asking and you will keep on getting; keep on looking and you will keep on finding; knock and the door will be opened. Everyone who asks, receives; all who seek, find; and the door is opened to everyone who knocks." (Luke 11:5-10) the most important message in this story that Jesus was trying to tell us is this: persistence is the key.

I felt this very strongly that when we go through serious problems in our life, no matter what, if we are serious with all our heart and our prayer life is in line with his will, he will answer us. Even if our faith is falling because we are giving our whole heart to him by our actions in prayer, surrender all to him. Something else has given me some strong and helpful advice I'd like to share: when we feel deep in despair, read the Book of Job. I've read this many times and it's helped me to understand God better. This will really help you too. Read Job when we feel really bad about ourselves or life that's going on around us!

Now I want you to try something and be real honest with yourself! You'll need an open heart and mind too. Go out in a field by yourself and listen quietly. Look around and see the clouds in the sky. Listen to the locust, and just listen. Do this for about an hour by yourself with no one else around, no radio blasting or any other noise. Just you. Look at the birds fly, or maybe at night look at the beautiful stars. Do this alone. Say, "Here I am, Jesus." Talk to him and then listen, listen, try this! Listen and you will hear a small voice. Say, "Here I am, Here I am." Listen and tell him what's on your mind! Go ahead; I want you to try this. We can go to Jesus Christ in our prayers. We don't have to go to anybody else. He is our prophet. In Mark 3:31-35, *"Jesus's mother and brother arrived at a crowded house where Jesus was teaching and they sent word for him to come out and talk with them. 'Your mother and brother are outside and want to see you' he was told. He replied, "Who is my mother? Who is my brother? Looking at everyone around him he said, 'these are my mother and brothers! Anyone who does God's will is my brother, and my sister, and my mother.'"*

You see, Jesus was telling all of us to come to Him. We are all his brother, sister and mother. He was also telling us that Mother Mary isn't that high up and that Jesus is the one we go to in our prayers. So Mother Mary doesn't need to intervene for us to get to Jesus. Nor do we need archbishops or cardinals or even the pope! Now I'm not saying that we don't need our pope because he is a very humble man who does a lot of good in the world ... I'm just saying we live in a broken world and when we're broken, we can go *straight to Jesus Christ!* We don't even need to confess our sins to a priest. Jesus is our prophet ...

God took an oath that Christ would always be a priest. Although he never said that of other priests. The Lord has sworn and will never change his mind: You are a priest forever, with the rank of Melchizedek. "Because of God's oath, Christ can guarantee forever the success of this new and better arrangement. Under the old arrangement, there had to be many priests, so that when the older ones died off, the system could still be carried on by others who took their places. But Jesus lives forever and continues to be a priest so that no one else is needed. He is able to save completely all who come to God through him. Since he will live forever; he will always be there to remind God that he has paid for their sins with his blood." (Heb. 7:20-25)

There was a period in my life where I kind of walked away from the Lord because of life issues but I never kept the Lord too far away and still never forgot my four miracles He did for me! Since 2011, I have been paying my tithes again for the Lord, I've been having miracle after miracle. The one day after a real hard day of work, I fell to my knees when I got home and asked the Lord, "Why? Why does it feel like I work in vain, listen to people complain all day and yell at you. When I think of all my investment I have in my retirement and I'm getting nothing on it or at least very little like ½ percent or less. Please tell me why this is so bad, Lord."

After being home for an hour and after being done praying, I just happened to open the Bible to Psalms 17:13-15: *"Lord, arise and stand against them. Push them back! Come save me from these men of the world whose only concern is earthly gain, these men whom you have filled with your treasures so that their children and grandchildren are rich and prosperous. But as for me, my contentment is not in wealth but in seeing you and knowing all is well between us. And when I awake in heaven, I will be fully satisfied, for I will see you face-to-face."*

This Song of David was written at the time when the Lord had delivered him from his many enemies including Saul. That's how the Lord wants us to be. Let's not worry about the problems of this world, money, and getting ahead in this life. "Let's live one day at a time" and keep our eyes on Jesus, and store our treasures in heaven where our heart is and someday we will awake in heaven and be fully satisfied for I will see him face-to-face. I look forward to this spiritual world we are all going into, not this present world. So how can we keep track of our life by doing these two principles Jesus said in Matthew 22:37, *"If you can remember these first two commandments out of Ten Commandments, you are obeying all ten of them. (1) Love the Lord your God with all your heart, soul, and mind and (2) love your neighbor as much as you love yourself. All these other commandments stem from these two laws.* You see because you wouldn't steal, lie, or murder your neighbor, you would just love them and they could trust you with everything." Everything! Love your neighbor means everybody. (You could be a true loyal friend!)

I'm thinking of this story in the Bible of King Saul and David: Saul was searching for David and wanted to kill him. David's intentions were the same but he was hiding from Saul; Saul went into the cave to relieve himself. *"Then David crept forward and quietly slit off the bottom of Soul's robe. But then his conscience began bothering him. 'I shouldn't have done it,' he said to his men. It is a serious sin to attack God's chosen king anyway? Afterwards when Saul left the cave, David came out of the cave and bowed low and yelled to Saul. 'My Lord, the King!' Later Saul called back, 'Is it really you, my son David?' Then he began to cry and said to David, 'You are a better man than I am for you have repaid me good for evil. Yes, you have delivered me into your hand, you didn't kill me.'"* (1 Sam. 24:4-6)

Now did you notice David's conscience was bothering him to do right? In Genesis 1:27, it says, *"God made man in his own image."* So, what is it? What are we doing? Why are we hurting one another? We are all special. We're all made by God and we need to listen to that small inner voice from God to do right! We are all fearfully and wonderfully made. *"Thank you for making me so wonderfully complex! It is amazing to think about. Your workmanship is marvelous—and how well I know it. You were there while I was being formed in utter seclusion! You saw me before I was born and scheduled each day of my life before I began to breathe. Every day was recorded in your Book."* (Psalm 139:14-16)

Let's just look at our eye. Light comes through an opening called the pupil which is the black circle in the center of the colored part of the eye. Just back of the pupil is a lens. This lens throws a picture on the retina at the back of the eyeball. We have millions of optic nerves in our eye which carries a message to the brain! Only God could make such a wonder as this. No man could ever perfect this wonderful eye with all the millions of nerves in it.

So when we have problems in our lives, we look at each other with compassion in our hearts. We all have faults in our lives and no one is perfect. We need to look this way toward others, the way God looks at us. God loves us even with our imperfections. I think of all these people in the world that have these special gifts from God without ever learning them. 1 Corinthians 13:1 tells us that: *"They could speak every language on earth or even heaven but they didn't love others, they would just be making noise. Or they had the gift of prophecy and knew everything about everything but didn't love others what good would that do? Even if I had the Gift of Faith so that I could speak to a mountain and make it move, I would still be worth nothing at all without love. Or if I gave everything I had to the poor and if I was burned alive for preaching the Gospel, but didn't love others, it would be of no value whatever."* So we need to be very careful how we live. All these special gifts come from God and should never put God on the back burner of our life and when we become rich and prosperous, we need to remember others that are lower than us. There is a responsibility here and let's never forget to thank God for everything even the food we eat.

I felt a pull from the Lord to write this book during the first week of February in 2015. When I broke the cross on the front of this book, I was bothered by it. So I prayed about this when I was resting on my bed after a hard day of work. We have a quilt on our bed that has squares with hundreds of designs. As soon as I was done praying about the broken cross, the first thing I saw was six broken crosses all in one of the squares! So I did feel confirmation from the Lord for the front cover when he told me before. There was another day I felt really sick following a day's hard work. My nose was just running and I lay on the bed praying and asked the Lord, "Do you love me?" I opened my eyes and the first thing I saw was my wadded up hanky that had many designs on it as it lay on the end table. It was a face smiling at me! Is it Jesus? I couldn't have reshaped that hanky to look like that in a million years.

The next couple of days, I was praying again about the wadded up hankie smiling at me and I was still thinking, if Jesus would show me another sign, this time I will write it down permanently because I lost the first one. Just as I was lying on my bed with my head on the pillow, as soon as I opened my eyes and saw it on my comforter. It had many leaves and flowers in the designs and I don't know how my eyes caught it. But as I squinted in a certain way, I saw a pattern of a person smiling at me. I was so amazed. So I wrote this down on a piece of paper.

Now I just felt the Lord impress upon me to tell everyone about this and that this has happened the second time too! Jesus was telling us when we feel we are not worthy and are sinners, the Lord looks at us and says, "0, but I love you more!" He says if we just get on our knees and go to him, he will gladly love us greatly and show us many miracles.

Let's go back to the events of my life. The pie factory sent me a letter advising me I no longer was a member of the union because they had been late with my grievances with the company twice so I was out of the union. The company said they could forgive the union for being late once but not twice. After the three months with the union, they let me go… So I ran into my parent's home and said, "What am I going to do now?" My dad said, "It's time to get a lawyer." The lawyer said we're taking it all the way to the Supreme Court. It seemed right after retaining a lawyer, the company finally started calling. They backed down and gave me back my job around mid-September of 1985. I got six months backpay and my seniority rights reinstated.

The lawyer told me if anyone harassed me on the job to give him a call. The first week I worked it went well. The next week my supervisor told me he wanted me to come in Tuesday at a certain time, so I did what I was told. After that I went back to my regular schedule for work on Wednesday. My supervisor saw me and said, "What are you doing here?" I told him "You said Tuesday!" The supervisor said, "No! You didn't follow my orders." So he said, "We'll see about this." He walked away and came back later. He had filled out a paper on me called a write up. "I put you on notice for not following orders." I just couldn't believe it! So I called my lawyer and he wrote the company a letter advising them to leave me alone. So the supervisor had to throw out the write up notice and he didn't bother me any-more. I'm thinking to myself, harassment on the job!

The summer of 1986, one of my friends called and asked if I wanted to pick him up on the way to a rock concert. He was really excited about it and I was thinking it might be fun. I had never been to one before and when we arrived there, I think there must have been five thousand people and the place was rockin'! My friend saw someone he knew and someone else. Then it was getting really wild! People were bringing in beer coolers and the next thing I saw was a fight! People were swearing, being cool when they saw each other. Then the concert started and it was so crowded and noisy.

I was there maybe an hour and very uncomfortable. I could tell my friend didn't want to leave so I asked him if one of his friends could take him home because I didn't want to be there anymore. He said, "Yes." So I couldn't wait to leave. I felt like I was in Sodom and Gomorrah. As soon as I opened the door from the building to leave, I kicked my feet from under me and dust flew from behind me. I thought to myself, "I can't even think to myself or even you, Jesus."

So the farther I walked in that long parking lot the better it was. Oh, it even made me cringe! As I was walking farther away it sounded like a loud murmur and it was getting quieter. I felt that God wasn't there. Getting into my car it was quiet and I could finally hear myself and the Lord. I drove home, turned the light off, got down on my knees and prayed. "Oh, dear Lord, I don't want this in my life. What an experience. Argh!

Years later, I was thinking about that rock concert and as I was thinking of it, I just happened to open my Bible to Ecclesiastes 7:1-4, *"A good reputation is more valuable than the most expensive perfume. The day one dies is better than the day he is born. It is better to spend your time at funerals than at festivals. For you are going to die and it is a good thing to think about it while there is still time. Sorrow is better than laughter. For sadness has a refining influence on us. Yes, a wise man think's much of death, while the fool thinks only of having a good time now."* Did we catch that phrase in the Bible? *"The day one dies is better than the day he is born,* so there is an encouragement in this next life we are going in!" It's a wonderful promise from God. Not to fear death, but walk right into it with excitement in our new life.

Oh, we should never forget this. This is such an important verse in the Bible. Isaiah 40 v 31: *"But they that wait upon the Lord shall renew their strength. They shall mount up with wings like an eagle. They shall run and not be weary; they shall walk and not faint."* Thank you Lord. We can learn so much from God's Word. When we have hard times in our life, let's get down on our knees and go to Jesus and also refer to the Bible! If the King James Version is too hard to read, go and buy the Living Version. Try doing this; it can help you understand the Bible better. The Living Version helped me to understand the Bible better.

Meanwhile, I've been working in that pie factory for over thirty-two years this year (2016) and it's been very hard in there. People have not been the nicest in there; it's been long hours and long days. Some people tell me factory work is not for them but if they are looking for a different job that makes them happy but doesn't pay the bills at home, isn't this job a necessity?

One day, I told my mom on the phone I didn't feel like going to church because I was very upset with certain people from work. I just didn't feel like it. I felt really, really bad—I could just cry. She told me, "That's when you really need to go to church." I'm glad I listened to her because that day and there have been many more of them when I didn't feel like going but did it anyway. I forced myself and I'm glad I did because I got such a message from the pastor that day. It's like the Lord talked right to me through him. Wow! I've found a verse that's helped me. *"Yet faith comes from listening to this good news—the good news about Christ."* (Rom. 10:17). This tells us we need church in our life *and* the Bible too … just pick it up and read it. You see, the Devil tells us in our mind not to go to church and he doesn't want us to read the truth!

I've also noticed something else about my four miracles. Two came from the New Testament as well as two from the Old Testament. I believe God was telling me that they are both very important and we should read both of them … Amen.

CHAPTER 9

Why Do We Live in a Broken World?

Why do we live in a broken world? What is the biggest question people ask? Why are people starving in this world? Who is responsible for this? In Luke 10:18, we're told, *"Yes, Jesus said. I saw Satan falling from heaven as a flash of lightning!"* In Isa 14:12-17, it says *"How you are fallen from heaven, O Lucifer, Son of the morning! How you are cut down to the ground-mighty though you were against the nations of the world for you said to yourself, 'I will ascend to heaven and rule the angels. I will take the highest Throne; I will preside on the mount of assembly far away in the north. I will climb to the highest heavens and be like the most high.' But instead, you will be brought down to the pit of hell, down to its lowest depth. Everyone there will store at you and ask, can this be the one who shocked the earth and the kingdoms of the world? Can this be the one who destroyed the world and made it into a shambles and demolished its greatest cities and had no mercy on his prisoners?"* Notice it says mighty though you were against the nations of the world. Now, mighty means pre-eminent which is superior to others (outstanding).

After my third miracle happened to me, I had this dark moment of doubt. I felt it in March 1985. I was thinking about Job in Job 2:2-6, *"Where have you come from? The Lord asked Satan. From patrolling the earth, Satan replied. 'Have you noticed my servant Job (or Karl)? Ha!' Satan said ... 'If I can convince him this is not real! This is just a coincidence? He will throw the Bible in the closet ... and say there is no God?' 'Go ahead,' the Lord said, 'AND see what he will do ...'"* Well. You know what I did: I just couldn't just quit! I had to push on ... AND I'm glad I did!

Now what I want to say about this is just because we get close to the Lord in our life doesn't mean Satan can't intervene in our life. In John 14:30-31, *Jesus was talking to his disciples telling them that he didn't have much time to talk to them. "... For the evil prince of this world approaches. He has no power over me, but I will freely do what the father requires of me so that the world will know that I love the father. Come let's be going."* For you see, Satan has the right to patrol the earth and he can bother us, even good Christian people that serve Jesus. It's up to us how we're going to live just like I said in the beginning of my book. This life is a test to see if we're going to be good or bad. Only you decide your outcome.

Through the years since I graduated from school, I always thought to myself that there must be a reason why I stayed at 4.31 my last five times in the 1600 meters. Was the Lord trying to tell me something about this number 431? Many years of going to work in the plant I went in at 1:00 a.m. and was very busy. We have a digital clock on the far end of the hall that you can barely see. It would say 4:31 not 4:30 and this has happened so many times. I also had too many circumstances where I was driving downtown in my busy moments in the car and the clock would say 4:31. Also I've been resting at home watching TV and just happened to look at my digital VCR player and it would say 4:31. At work I got my Hi/Lo license and was changing my battery. There were probably ten of them in a row and somehow I grabbed number 431. This number has happened so many times in my life even when I'm on vacation. There were other times where I wanted to do classified jobs so I could pay my house bills better, etc. And my supervisor didn't have confidence in me and I always had to prove myself to him on these certain jobs and he would later stand in the hallway with someone else smirking at me, I did a baker mixer II job which means I ran depositor on a line all by myself, which required to run about 23,000 Boston pies, also the other room where I did mixing other days, where the pies came out from BMI (the oven). There was one day I had to get my temperature gage from quality control room and they had a handful of gage, I need one for the back of the oven because I had to take temperature every three times every hour for the center, west and east end, plus weigh five times an hour and making sure everything is all right. Anyway, I walked in the quality control room to get my temperature gage. They had a bunch of them, one for the hot gages, one for the cold gages, and all on separate trays in the room. And I happened to grab H-431. This has happened so many times.

So for many years, I have searched and looked in the Bible for something to do with 431 and I couldn't find anything. Finely one day this summer of 2015, I happened to open the Bible to one page that I had highlighted. I read Proverbs 8:33-35 that says, *"Listen to my counsel-oh don't refuse it and be wise. Happy is the man who is so anxious to be with me that he watches for me daily at my gates, or waits for me outside my home! For whoever finds me finds life and wins approval from the Lord.* " Oh isn't that what we need to do. He's telling us to keep our hearts right with him and keep seeking him and watch for him daily while we keep our eyes open for his gates. Amen. Then I just looked at the page number in my Bible and it was open to page 431! This is what Jesus wanted me to know! I felt the Lord wanted me to tell you this before I finished this book.

Oh, dear Lord Jesus, my love is so deep in you because you first loved me! I want to tell everyone in the world how great the Lord is! And what I've been through with my *four miracles* and in my life. *"Always as for me and my house we will serve the Lord."* (Josh. 24:15).

Thank you, Jesus Christ, for saving my life that day in 1985! I give you all the glory! Jesus, Lamb of God! Worthy is your name!

CHAPTER 10

Victory through Jesus Christ

I give Jesus Christ the entire honor for helping me write this book! I will never forget!

When we feel hopeless and alone, the world is closing in on us; we are hurt or scared and it feels like we are in a dark tunnel and can't see that light at the other end—let's get on our knees and pray to Jesus Christ, in his name and just surrender everything to him. He loves everybody in this world. We can always call 9-1-1 with him and we can go to him right now! Yes, we can. We have this wonderful channel and he can go where ever we are in this life. If we just give him our *all*, we have this, personal connection with him and Jesus will rescue us. He shed great drops of blood on the cross for everyone in this whole world! He is on the right hand of God … if we just pray to him with a serious heart. We can be trapped in a dark, dark cave *and* he will listen to you and hear our cries—and give us victory!

He will show us the truth! For Jesus said, this prayer, Matthew 11 verses 27-30, *everything has been entrusted to me by my father. Only the father knows the son and the father is known only by the son and by those to whom the son reveals him. Come to me and I will give you rest-all of you who work so hard beneath a heave yoke. Wear my yoke for it fits perfectly and let me teach you; for I am gentle and humble, and you shall find rest for your souls; for I give you only light burdens.*

Yes, let us go back to church and learn wisdom from the Lord by listening to a pastor at church.

Our victory is in Jesus Christ! My disability is his victory! Amen! He is the answer for everything. I give all honor, praise, and glory to Jesus!

God is so real. He was there for me when I needed him. The hardships in my life brought me to being broken so that the Lord could heal me. I have the Lord in my life now and I plan to keep him there. He brought me here at this point in my life where I can witness to you right now. You, too, can have this wonderful joy in your life. I believe He can change your life—just like he did mine!

"Yes" are we still going through the motions in our Christian life. Just being so so! having Christ serve us instead of serving him. It says in Hebrews 5:12

That we have been a Christian for a long time and we are staying this same old Christian we're we still need to be taught over and over again, we are still like babies who can only drink milk and were not old enough for solid food and when a person is still living on milk, it shows he isn't very far along in his Christian life. And doesn't know the difference between right and wrong.

He's still a baby Christian! and we won't ever be able to eat solid spiritual food until we learn the deeper things of God's word, until we become better Christian's and learn right from wrong by practicing doing right.

Yes I used to be a follower in my life but something changed in my life about being a leader for Jesus Christ. Now!

Let's look at this event in the bible.
—Acts 1:9

After Christ resurrection and when he was leaving the disciples into the sky on the mount of olives and the disciples were standing there staring and were straining their eyes trying to get a last glimpse of him when suddenly two white robed men we're standing there among them and said men of Galilee, why are you still staring at the sky?

Jesus has gone up to heaven and some day just as he went, he will return!"

Yes what are we doing??

Why are we still staring at the sky?

Let's get busy by telling other's about Jesus great love for us. Amen:

LET'S STAND UP FOR JESUS!
'YES' STAND UP FOR JESUS!!

Let's have this deep walk for him and serving others.

Before I close this book, can we remember these last important thoughts. Let's set a goal in our life to keep in constant mind how Jesus Christ would want us to be. *"To be more humble toward others."* Yes, let's try really hard to have more love and peace in this world. We are having way too much violence in this world … *"Yes"* so let's remember to do our best *"always." To have a clear conscious toward God and people* (Act's 24:16) and we can go straight to Jesus Christ in our prayers and God will hear us also …

I must also add the Holy Spirit is very important to us. For when I had my hardship in this life "He was my comforter." So all three work together. God, the Son, and the Holy Spirit. "Trinity."

Yes, you see when Jesus died on the cross, he saved all of us. He bought us with a great price so when we're broken, we can all come to him. He is our Savior! He is the truth the Light, and the Way the only way! Let's wake up and go to him! *Jesus Christ* …

Just by how I was raised, I want to give special credit to both my parents and My Special Ed. Teacher, Mrs. Kathy Woods, for the strictness they gave me. I wouldn't be where I am today without it. They taught me no matter what, to stand up to this life I was facing.

I stayed with my job all these years, bought my own house, and now I am the note owner. I got married in 2000 to my wonderful wife, Mellissa. I want to give special thanks to her for helping me when I was stuck on certain words. Also, special thanks to Avis Ward for transcribing my notes and listening to me.

PS: this whole book is authentic; everything about me and my belief in Jesus Christ. Karl A. Olson.

ABOUT THE AUTHOR

I was born and raised in Traverse City, Michigan, and have attended Bayview Wesleyan Church all my life. My wife and I love to travel and the only baby we have is a pug, Nemo! I'm still working in a pie factory. It has been thirty-two years now (2016). I love to walk around my sub and think about the Lord.

Yes. Let us keep our faith in deep Reverence for the Lord.